1On

A Journey to the Magical Other

for Shauna

[signature]

find your inner music to carry you on your journey

On The Broken Road

A Journey to the Magical Other

Healing the Soul, Skyclad: Volume 2

Robert G. Longpré

Retired Eagle Books

Revised Edition, March, 2015

Dedication

This story is my gift to my three adult children, Noelle, Natasha and Dustin who are now parents busy with the raising of their own children, busy living their own stories. I also dedicate this story to my wife, Maureen, my Magical Other, who has shared this life journey with me through our own improbable stories of love and life for more than forty years.

Robert G. Longpré

"whatever reality may be, it will to some extent be shaped by the lens through which we see it". – James Hollis, Jungian Analyst, The Middle Passage, 1993.

Retired Eagle Books
Box 423
Elrose, Saskatchewan,
Canada S0L 0Z0

ISBN-13: 978-1508872009

Table of Contents

Foreword

This is a story of a young man, a folk-music playing flower-child of the late sixties who hitch-hikes across Canada at the time of Woodstock with his young lady love. He is the quintessential Flower Child, the precursor of the hippies of the early 70s. As all good stories go, love is lost and the young man finds himself again wandering across Canada and north-western USA in search of healing for his broken heart.

In a way, this is a mythological tale in a modern setting, with the hero wandering through darkness, fighting the forces of evil, battling the complexes of life and monsters of archetypal proportions, a story that is told over and over again in our small personal dramas in our ordinary lives.

The characters of this tale are real, just the names have been changed. Yet, in spite of that, no writer can recreate a character in a story, even one that is objectively real, without investing a part of who he or she is, as well as the lived experience the author has of the others. As a result, one could easily say with some validity that besides being real people, all the characters in this story, as in all stories, are simply a collection of inner voices that live within each of us, and the outer voices that surround us.

The places such as towns, streets and other features of geography are real. The Strawberry Fields Festival as Mosport Freeway near Toronto in 1970 was a real event I attended with the named acts in this story actually in attendance as performers. Everything else is a product of active imagination and my memories placed here as a story.

Healing the Soul, Skyclad

This is the second book in a series of stories that takes the idea of being clothed by the sky, being au naturel, as a means of healing trauma. The main character of this story is introduced is a scene where he is nude. His nudity is an unconscious response to trauma, a response that is healing on different levels. I use the term *skyclad* intentionally because it has a spiritual connotation that goes back to the beginnings of humanity's response and relationship to itself and to its creator.

Our creation story begins with humans in a state of perfection and holiness, unclothed in the Garden of Eden. A traumatic act caused this state of holiness to be broken. Feeling the shame of this trauma, and all victims of trauma feel shame, humans hid. We are told that we can return to the Garden of Eden, to heaven by doing the work to regain our innate holiness that remains within us. The real journey we all take is about healing the soul and regaining the purity in which we were created. Our creator knew us as perfect and good when there was nothing to hide and nothing to hide behind. Heaven isn't clothing optional, nor was the Garden of Eden. You have something to hide? You can't get in.

Trauma takes many forms: physical trauma, relationship trauma, psychological trauma, emotional trauma, and identity trauma. Trauma is real and it marks one for life. One can't wish it away, or drown it with alcohol, or wipe it out with drugs, or erase it with therapy, or ignore it by filling life to the brim with things and activity. Rather than ignore trauma, we learn to see it as it is. Only then can we make choices to learn from the trauma and heal.

Part One

You Can't Go Home

Chapter One

This story continues on where the last story, <u>Broken Boy</u>, left off with Benjamin and Céline in Toronto after having fled from their problems in Ottawa. Unlike book one, I won't be interrupting the story very often with my commentary from a point in time more than forty years after the event. Now, the story of a <u>Broken Boy</u> continues as he finds himself on a <u>Broken Road</u>. In this second book, I am switching to having this story of myself as a young man, being told in the third person, putting some objective distance between myself in my sixties and my younger self.

~

Benjamin and Céline met Americans in Toronto, young men who had said "No" to the idea of going to die in Vietnam; Americans who played music, some of them who would one day become famous musicians in famous bands. They stayed for about a week getting to meet people and to get lost in the crowds. Ben was glad that he knew how to play well enough so as to not be laughed out of various jam sessions, especially when one of the groups he got to play with had already begun to be noticed in the recording industry. But this wasn't what Benjamin and Céline needed, this time in Yorkville was just a rest stop. Seeing the drunks in Bloor Street Park, the stoned kids spaced out and sitting almost unaware of their bodies, told Benjamin that this wasn't where he belonged. And Céline was beginning to draw darker images again. It was time to leave.

Before leaving, Benjamin picked up a used backpack that someone had been abandoned in the house they were staying in. They found an abandoned sleeping bag and packed a small bit of food to go with their few items of clothing, none of it costing them any money. Everything they had was given to them knowing that the givers would somehow get what they needed in return in the future. It was a good thing as money wasn't abundant. Benjamin and Céline hadn't waited until Ben's payday before leaving. At the time money seemed the least important thing to worry about. They had reacted out of anger and fear and despair.

They headed north not knowing where they would end up or even why they were heading in that direction. Benjamin didn't want to go to the States when it seemed that all the good people were leaving that place. Benjamin and Céline hitchhiked stopping where their rides stopped usually finding other young people who had found themselves at the same place. It seemed as though there were homes or rooms open for those lost on the roads. Céline got her period the day after leaving Toronto. She was in a panic as she saw how little money they had and it seemed stupid to waste that little bit of money on sanitary napkins. As she panicked Benjamin thought of letting her use his underwear as her napkins as they could be washed and no harm would be done to them. Benjamin learned to go commando under his clothing and not be self-conscious about it.

They slept in the sleeping bag together. At first Benjamin slept with his pants on so as to not embarrass or stress out Céline. She clung close to him, closer than anyone had even been to him before, needing him even in her sleep. Before going to sleep she would arrange her clothing in a neat pile so that they wouldn't be too wrinkled for the next day. With her small breasts, Céline never wore a bra. As she clung to Benjamin as they lay side by side, they would touch each other and kiss, hungry for more. But since she was menstruating and still afraid of more, that is where it stopped with passions unfilled.

One early morning, Benjamin woke up with his pants wet with semen forcing him to slip out of the sleeping bag made for one person but able to hold two small people, and try to rub the pants dry. Slipping out of the sleeping bag, he removed his pants to wipe as much of the moisture off. While still nude, he found the iron and ironing board and was trying to press the wrinkles out of the pants as well as remove the last traces of moisture when Céline came to stand beside him. She told Benjamin that from now on he shouldn't wear his pants to bed. As Benjamin stood there, naked from the waist down, he told her that he had no underwear to put on for sleeping. She smiled and said that it didn't matter as he was beautiful without clothes on, and it was okay for him to sleep beside her in the nude. She called Benjamin beautiful as he stood there, exposed. And, he could see that she meant it.

Benjamin and Céline continued the journey which took them to Port William. Their last ride was with a man heading home from work, a man not too much older than they were. As he neared the turnoff to his house, he asked Benjamin and Céline if they would go to his house for a warm meal before continuing on their journey. Benjamin and Céline were getting used to the fact that people were nice and kind so they said yes with no hesitation.

When they at his home, his young wife treated the two hitch-hikers as friends, as if this was an everyday occurrence, having her husband bring home strangers for supper. She refused to let Benjamin and Céline leave after supper saying that they should stay the night and use her washing machine to freshen up their clothing. They gave Benjamin and Céline a bed in the spare room and some clothes to use while their clothes were getting washed. Because they were getting to sleep in a bed, Benjamin and Céline put the sleeping bag out to air, turned inside out. Benjamin took a bit of extra time to try to clean up the faint stickiness that was inside the sleeping bag.

While Benjamin played some guitar that evening, as an

attempt to say thank you, the man's wife took Céline aside and gave her a few sanitary napkins to last for the rest of her cycle. Benjamin and Céline decided to accept the couple's invitation and stayed with them for two nights so that their clothes could dried and be ironed. Then, with their bags packed with a few more clothes than when they had left Toronto, Benjamin and Céline headed off, heading west.

Getting rides wasn't difficult in the summer of 1969. There was something about a young couple, with a backpack, a small suitcase, and a guitar that gives people a sense of "it's safe to stop and give these kids a ride," especially when they were relatively well dressed and didn't look like hippies or druggies. From Port Arthur going west, they didn't stay at the homes of others or with other young travelers – they stopped and slept in small fields under the stars. It was summer, later summer, and warm. At least until the night they stopped in Golden, B.C.

They had stopped at an Esso gas station near the entrance to this mountain city and decided to camp out on the side of the hill behind the gas station's restaurant after they had eaten a small meal. The stars made an indescribable light show as they cuddled into the sleeping bag. It didn't take too long before they finally fell asleep in the darkness.

The cold mountain air woke Céline in the middle of the night and she began to panic in the intense darkness. She was sure she had heard wolves and thought they were going to kill her and Benjamin. Ben tried to reason with her as he held her tight giving as much of his warmth as he could. But the panic, just got worse. She broke out of his arms and started to run down the hill naked and barefoot. Benjamin caught her and told her she needed to get her clothes on promising that as soon as they could pack up, he would then take her down the hill to the gas station where whey would find another ride and get away from the wolves, away from her night fears.

Céline calmed down enough so that Benjamin could lead her back up the slope to the small tent. They both put on their clothing and then walked carefully as they could in the darkness back down the side of the mountain to the lights of the gas station. Back at the gas station they stopped long enough for coffee and to wait and to ask around for a ride from one of the truckers heading west. They were lucky as one driver told them he had room for the two of them and that he was going all the way to Vancouver.

Vancouver was now their destination. Benjamin remembered that his Uncle Ben and Aunt Jennie were now living in Vancouver and that if needed, Céline and he could get a bit of help from them. Benjamin knew that the running had to stop, that he needed to get a job and that they needed a place to stay warm with fall and winter not all that far away.

The trucker stopped for a meal in Hope. B.C. While they were having more coffee and a small meal, a young man in his late twenties or early thirties had noticed Céline. He came over to the table and began to talk with Céline. He had noticed Céline's art folder and he wondered if he could see her paintings and drawings. He told Céline that he was an art collector. He hoped that he could perhaps buy one or two if they would fit into his collection. Céline got excited; this was her dream, to be a successful artist. After viewing her work, the man pointed to two of them and offered Céline money, more money than either Benjamin or Céline had left, enough money for them to get started in Vancouver. Céline sold him the two drawings and began talking animatedly about her desire to work with acrylics and oils.

As the conversation continued, the truck driver told Céline and Benjamin that he was leaving to go on to Vancouver if we wanted to continue going there with him. Hearing that, the man who just bought the drawings told them that they could travel on to Vancouver with him if they wanted, and that they could even stay in his house until getting their own place. Benjamin hesitated as he was getting uncomfortable with the attention this stranger was giving to them, especially the focused attention on Céline. It sounded too good to be true and Benjamin had learned long before to be wary of things that appeared too good to be true. There was something about him that Benjamin just didn't trust.

However, when the stranger added that they could pay him for staying at his house by painting murals on the walls of the attic room in the house. He said he would let them stay in the attic, as a way to pay him rent. He would even provide the paints that Céline needed, both acrylics and oil paints. Céline said yes, that they would go with him. She hadn't asked Benjamin; she just assumed that he would follow. The truck driver gave a small shake of his head as he heard Céline's decision. It was as if he agreed with Ben's doubts. Céline was too excited about the chance to do something with her talents, to paint. She began to dream of living an artist's life in Vancouver.

Later that morning Céline and Benjamin arrived at the young man's house, a decent older looking house that had moss growing on the cedar shakes of the roof. The house wasn't large, but it wasn't too small either. It didn't look like the house of someone to be wary of at all. Benjamin began to think maybe they would be okay here until he could get a real job and take care of Céline in their own home. The man pointed to the gable window looking out onto the street telling the two of them that is where they could stay if they decided to take him up on his offer. He was adamant that needed to see the room before making their decision. He told them to stay the night and let him know the next day.

Céline could barely sit still in her excitement – an artist's garret, just like what one hears about and reads about from the lives of famous painters who lived in Paris and New York. When the man showed them the room, he told them that he wanted floor-to-ceiling murals on two walls, the taller walls. He told them they could paint anything that they wanted using any kind of paint they wanted to use. He would buy the art materials since the two murals were going to be his in the end anyway. Benjamin suggested perhaps they could use acrylic paints so that the pictures would dry faster and not give problems in the damp air. Céline stubbornly wanted to use oil paint.

Before the ideas were out of their mouths the man said, they could try using both media and decide as they went along. He suggested that Benjamin start on one wall while Céline worked on the opposite wall, both of them using different media. The idea surprised both Céline and Benjamin, as he didn't see myself as an artist, nor did Céline. This was her territory. Benjamin could detect a hint of resentment and anger in her eyes.

Seeing Céline's expression, the young man was quick to suggest to Céline that they should give it a try. He told Céline that she could always paint over my botched work when her wall was completed. She was the boss, and it was her decision in the end what would be on the walls. Those were the magic words Céline needed to hear. She was the boss, the artist in charge. Céline said yes, yes, yes. Her face beamed with a big grin. The two young easterners dropped their things into the room and then went to an art supply shop with the man to buy a large selection of brushes and paints. The shop wasn't far from the house and the shop owner was told that when they needed more paints and other supplies, it was okay to put them on a bill which the man then would pay later.

The man then showed Benjamin and Céline where they could buy their groceries at a nearby store. Benjamin began to realize that though they would live rent free, he would need to get a job. It took money to buy groceries and even though they now had some money from the sale of two of Céline's drawings, it wasn't going to last all that long. He still needed to get a job. Later that evening when they were alone, Benjamin brought up the idea of him looking for a real job. Céline was against his leaving her alone to look for work. She convinced Benjamin to wait for a while before looking for a job as she wanted him to paint with her in the house.

For the next two weeks they did nothing but talk of scenes and try to bring the scenes to the walls with pencil sketches. Céline suggested that they wear clothing when they painted so that they didn't ruin them with paint. Knowing that they didn't have money to spend on clothing; that what little money they did have was needed for food, Benjamin agreed. So began a different way of living in the attic of the house in Vancouver. They lived and worked without wearing clothes, only putting them on when they got invited for a meal on the main floor of the house or to a meal at a nearby restaurant.

Surprisingly, it wasn't hard to make the shift from clothed to nude for both Céline and Benjamin. Sometimes while Benjamin worked on the scenes Céline had sketched, she would be working with charcoal on sketches of Benjamin rather than working on the scenes for her wall. She would draw him while he painted, as he sat quietly reading while leaning against a wall, or while he was playing his guitar for her. Her drawings left nothing to the imagination while yet evoking more than what could be seen in a mirror.

In spite of her drawings of him, Benjamin began to notice that she was avoiding the work on the painting of her wall. He also saw that she was again retreating into herself, retreating into silence. He sensed that she was starting to drift back into a depression but didn't know what to do about it, what to do to help her. All he knew was that she panicked if he went out of the attic room without taking her with him.

Benjamin's mural was just about done when the man dropped in to see what progress had been made. He didn't make any comments about seeing the two of them working in the nude. Benjamin wondered if perhaps he thought it was normal for artists to paint while nude. The man was excited about what he saw, all of the designs that were outlined by Céline the two walls. The fact that the painting which Benjamin had done was not done all that well didn't matter to him. He loved the colors and the rawness of the images. He noticed that the wall in oils that Céline was working on was coming along very slowly, yet he stood in awe of what was done and what images were sketched in yet to be painted. The very dark colors and scenes brought out images of a private hell were powerful. He spoke with wonder of seeing Dante's inferno in living color. Benjamin's crude efforts were just that, more of a paint-by-number guide than it was about real painting. Céline's wall was pure emotion, pure art.

The man said very little as he took it all in. When he finally found his voice, he decided that what they were doing was worth more than free rent. He left two hundred dollars on the table by the door and then left them alone to continue their projects. Céline went to the money and looked at it and smiled. She knew she had earned this money. Then she began to cry. There was no more painting that day. She cried and Benjamin held her. She cried for a long time, long into the night until fatigue had her finally descend into a fitful sleep just as dawn was beginning to break.

The work continued. Every time Benjamin stopped to watch Céline painting, he saw her think before she lifted her brush, taking a cloth to wipe out an idea she didn't like. She stood there studying her work totally unconscious of her naked body.

As he watched her, sometimes he could feel an erection begin to grow. Wearing nothing while looking at a beautiful young woman who loved him and his body, he suffered as making love to her was denied, at least for now. Benjamin ached for her to touch him, to hold him, to make love with him. Céline could sense Benjamin's and his attention and she would turn around and see his erection and a sadness in his eyes. Then she would put the brush down, come over and kiss him, look him in the eyes and tell him how much she loved him, how much she trusted him; she loved how he respected her need to not have intercourse. Then they would kiss and caress each other. The ache from being denied more, rose within Benjamin and then she would stroke my hair and say it was alright as he cried. It was her moment to care for him.

They were in Vancouver almost a month before Benjamin called his Uncle Ben and Aunt Jennie. The man at the house was creeping out Benjamin and Céline as he would often come into the room while they painted, more interested in seeing them paint naked than to check on their progress. Benjamin and Céline lived naked and painted naked within the attic as clothing was stored in safekeeping. The man would pretend come in to check out how they were doing, but he only had eyes for Céline. Each time he came, he brought in a bag of fresh vegetables and fruit and he would give Céline some money. Because of the fruit and vegetables, they didn't need to spend much of the money and rarely had to go out at all. Each time the man gave her the money, he made sure to say that "she" had more than earned every cent. It was as if Benjamin had become invisible and had contributed nothing. Benjamin began to hate him and his money and his house.

It wasn't long before the man began to come into the attic nude. Seeing him nude in "their" space, Céline was feeling disturbed by his presence, by his apparent obsession with seeing Céline nude. It wasn't seeing him naked that was creepiest, it was the way held his body and the reason for his nudity as though trying to position himself so that Céline would notice his penis. Benjamin was sure that the man had stroked himself enough to engorge his penis just before entering so that it would be larger and fuller, hard to miss, especially with the poses he took as he stood staring at Céline and pretending to be talking to both of them.

Then the man saw the drawings on the wall of Benjamin, the nude portraits that Céline continued to draw using charcoal. He went closer to study them before turning to look at Benjamin who felt like he was being judged as inferior man. The man studied the drawings, then glanced at Benjamin's limp penis with a look of pathetic distain. His look of distain only confirmed what Benjamin had often been told, that he really wasn't that much of a man. Was this the reason why Céline couldn't make love to him? Was he not enough of a man in her eyes?

Turning back to Céline, the man asked her if she would use his face rather than mine for these portraits since we would eventually be gone and the paintings and drawings would stay. He also wondered if she could make the penis look a little larger like his, not small like Benjamin's.

Céline was becoming more and more afraid of the man. She began to imagine that he was a serial killer, that he was just waiting for the right moment before he raped her and then chopped both of them up into small pieces. If he wasn't a serial killer, then he was a pervert. She was sure of it. She wanted Benjamin to get her out of the house, away from this sick man. She knew that they now had to leave, that this wasn't really the life that they were supposed to live.

Ben and Jennie were glad to hear from the two young runaways, that is to say, they were glad to hear from Benjamin as they didn't know Céline. Benjamin's aunt and uncle invited Benjamin and his girlfriend to stay with them for a while until they found their own place. Benjamin didn't tell them that he and Céline had been in Vancouver almost a month already. It was mid-September, still warm and sunny as Benjamin introduced Céline to Ben and Jennie. They fell in love with her immediately. Ben told his nephew that he had never thought young Benjamin could ever have such a beautiful young woman as his partner.

The two guests stayed for a week. Benjamin would go out during the day in search of a job while Céline sat in the apartment because of her fears. Céline and Benjamin were back to living an almost normal life wearing clothing except for when they spent the night together in the guest bed. Most nights when they went to bed, Céline would lay in Benjamin's arms with her head on his chest, a woman-child, innocent and vulnerable. Benjamin would lie still so as not to disturb her sleep, protecting her by drawing her even closer when she got restless in her sleep, a restlessness born from her dreams.

There were nights when Céline needed his touch, nights when she needed to feel more like a woman than a child. She would look at Benjamin then at his penis and then gently touch it. Then, Benjamin would touch her and she responded with the smallest of noises. There was no trace of love making, no semen stains in sheets, no used tissue holding the evidence of intercourse, because there was no intercourse.

One afternoon, Céline went with Benjamin to Gastown where Benjamin hoped he could find a coffee house where he could play some music and get a few dollars in return. Gastown was filled with young people, another Yorkville, only more on the edge. They met a few young couples who asked them to come to their commune. When they were told that there was no sex allowed in the commune, that it was a Christian commune,

Céline agreed that they should go and discover what it was about. With a place to go to, the two returned and told Ben and Jennie that they had found a place of their own to stay in, a place with other young people like themselves. Benjamin was sure that his aunt and uncle were relieved to see the two of them leave. A week was long enough.

The Christian commune was a strange place, a very strange community of young people mostly the same age. It seemed as if no one really worked. When Benjamin asked where the money came from for the food to feed so many people, he was told that most of them were collecting either welfare or unemployment insurance.

The place was a shifting whirl of gatherings for prayers, singing, and bible study. Yet in Benjamin's opinion, it didn't seem that many understood the words written in the Bible. Within the commune, it was evident that a few were the controlling figures dominating the whole group while trying to mold everyone else into a set belief system in spite of the words in the Bible. Céline was enthusiastic about the place and the people they found there. As she saw it, all the young men and women who had gathered together there had made a vow of purity, a vow of virginity, which made the place a sanctuary of safety. It was the surprise at seeing a few of the members engaged in sex and the exorcism that finally got to Céline.

One evening in early October, a group of girls had gathered around Céline while Benjamin had been talking about auras with a few others guys and girls in the common room. The girls had noticed a growing quietness in Céline, a quietness that had her withdrawing into a slight depression. In the commune, attempts to withdraw away from the group were viewed with suspicion. Benjamin had learned that it was better to argue rather than sit off in his own corner, for in arguments the others had hope to convert the uncertain. In the collective opinion, retreat into silence was putting oneself in danger of being seduced by Satan.

Before Benjamin had noticed the group around Céline, the young women had already placed their hands on Céline's head and were praying loudly asking for the demon of darkness to leave her. They were calling on Jesus to show Céline the light. Céline started screaming alerting Benjamin to the seriousness of the situation. He quickly rushed to Céline's side and broke up the activity while taking her out of the house to find a quiet and safe spot down the road.

Céline continued to scream and cry until she was too spent to scream any longer. With her screams now quiet, Benjamin took her to a nearby restaurant from which he called his Aunt Jennie who had experience as a psyche nurse in Montreal, for some help. With her advice, Benjamin rushed Céline to the hospital where they met both Jennie and his Uncle Ben. Céline was admitted to the hospital with a nervous breakdown. With the help of drugs, the doctors were able to stabilize Céline's condition. Finding out that Céline's family was in eastern Canada, they recommended her return there where she could then get needed long term care. The medications could only do so much.

Over the next few days, Benjamin, with the help of Jennie and Ben, made arrangements to take Céline back to Ottawa as Céline's mother needed to follow up on Céline's care. Jennie told Benjamin that Céline would need a lot of care for a long time and that he couldn't do this on his own, especially as Benjamin didn't have a place for to live, or a job to support both of himself and Céline in the process. Besides, Céline like Benjamin, was still considered a minor. Since they weren't married, Céline's mother had the only real authority in making health decisions.   Borrowing two hundred dollars from his Uncle Ben, young Benjamin bought train tickets to Ottawa.

Finally, with arrangements and phone calls to Ottawa made, Céline and Benjamin left Vancouver to return home, both of them more broken than when they had left Ottawa two months earlier.

Chapter Two

Not knowing what to do next, he has returned to his parents' home in the countryside. He hadn't been able to fall asleep in the old house his parents had moved to just three years earlier, and like other times when he was feeling helpless, he had retreated to this small meadow in a wooded area far enough from the house, behind the old barn, where he could be alone. It was his safe haven, his sanctuary where he often retreated to when he was upset, when things were rough. This retreat into the treed pasture began in the spring of his seventeenth year, eight months after the death of his maternal grandmother.

Benjamin couldn't remember what it was, exactly that sent him in search of a safe place, in search of sanctuary. Sometimes he simply sat there, in the sunshine and disappeared into books or into poetry. But always, when he entered his sanctuary, his holy place, he needed to be nude. It was as if he was entering the Garden of Eden, striving to somehow return to unconscious innocence. And this time, in early October of his twentieth year, he abandoned his clothing in a pile next to the tree in search of healing his broken heart.

It was chilly and Benjamin hugged himself into a tight ball in order to find some warmth. The idea of putting his clothes back on hadn't entered his mind. He had discovered this small opening in the wooded area two and a half years earlier, in the first spring that his family had lived at this old farmyard a few miles outside of Ottawa. He didn't remember what had happened that sent him out of the house in search of sanctuary, a place where he could nurse his wounds; and it didn't even matter. There had always been things happening that wounded him. Usually it was his father, Laurent, who was responsible for the wounding. It was because of his father that Benjamin had left home two months earlier taking Céline with him as they headed west in hopes of building a new life for both of them.

Benjamin felt the pricks of twigs and a bits of stone as he huddled naked on the ground, hugging his knees in the late hours of the night, just before the approach of dawn. Tears were slowly tracing a path down his cheeks; there were still a few of them left though he had been silently weeping for some time as he huddled as though trying desperately to hold the bits and pieces left of his broken heart.

His mind kept going over and over again the scene from yesterday afternoon at the Ottawa General Hospital, the moment when he saw Céline being wheeled off into the elevator flanked by her sister Carmen, her mother and her step-father. Céline's mother was staring at Benjamin with undisguised hatred. Benjamin had wanted to go with them as Céline was taken to her room in the psych ward; but, her mother was adamant that he would not be permitted to see her at all, at any time. She blamed him for her having to be hospitalized.

In despair, Benjamin sought out Dr. Michaels. He needed to talk to him. Benjamin had already talked with Dr. Michaels who was a psychologist, earlier in the afternoon when Benjamin had taken Céline to the hospital. Benjamin had told the doctor of the events in Vancouver that had led to him bringing her to the hospital in Ottawa. Knowing that the doctor needed more information if he was to help her, Benjamin told the doctor of the history of sexual abuse by her step-father and the emotional abuse by her mother and of Céline's frequent descents into darkness which she had disclosed to him over the summer. Benjamin showed the doctor a few of the drawings made by Céline that told of that inner darkness, and he told him of how Céline had mentally collapsed while in a Jesus freak commune in Vancouver just a few days earlier and how he had taken her to the hospital in Vancouver where he found out that she needed some long-term psychiatric care. Borrowing some money for train fare, Benjamin then took Céline home to Ottawa and straight to the hospital.

Doctor Michaels talked about the legal requirement of having to contact Céline's mother. It was the law. He wasn't happy with the law, especially when it was frequently the parents who were the cause of a youth having to be admitted to hospitals for trauma, physical and psychological trauma. The doctor was gentle as he listened to Benjamin explain what he knew of her abuse as a child and the events since Benjamin had met her. The doctor seemed impressed that someone his age could already be this mature and wise enough to reach out for help.

As the sky began to show a thin thread of light, Benjamin felt the chill increase and became aware of the twigs that were digging into his butt. He stood up and put on his pants and tee-shirt and slipped on his cheap sandals. He knew that he had to return to the house and gather his things together. He had to leave again though he wasn't too sure where he would go yet. He wanted to go back to Vancouver, but he didn't want to leave Ottawa either as he still hoped that somehow, Céline would be allowed to see him again. Making his way down the path that lead to the old farm yard, he saw the colors of dawn as the trees were replaced by cornfields and pastures. He stood still and gazed at the sky and felt a small Benjamin of hope begin to grow within himself.

Entering the silent house, Benjamin went to his old room just off the dining room, a room that had once been a pantry. It was a very small room, but in a house with nine children, having his own room was priceless.

The house was old and smelled musty. Aside from Benjamin's

little room, the main floor contained a large kitchen, dining room and living room. A room had been added on behind the kitchen quite a few years earlier, before his family had moved into the house; now, it served as pantry and storage room, and during the winter, a play room for the younger kids. Near the front entrance there was a small bathroom that held only a small sink along and a toilet. The stairs leading to the second level were accessed from the dining room and rose up over Benjamin's room. Benjamin remembered how he had helped his mother and father do some major renovation work with the dining room and living room which is where they entertained extended family, usually his father's side of the family, the French side. His mother's side was English, stiff and dour people for the most part.

Upstairs, there were three bedrooms; two for Benjamin's eight brothers and sisters, and his parent's bedroom. The two older girls and the two youngest boys were in the smaller of the two bedrooms for children. There were two sets of bunk beds and two narrow tall dressers in the room which was next to the parental bedroom. The bathroom stood between the girls' room and the boy's room. In the bedroom for the boys, there a double bed and a cot for the three older boys. These two bedrooms on the second floor were in need of new flooring and paint. But, it was doubtful that the work would ever be done. Benjamin's parents' bedroom had been remodeled and was painted in bright colors. The baby, a girl, slept in their room which, in spite of the renovations and color, was always in a state of disarray.

Benjamin's mother had long ago given up caring about her house and Benjamin didn't blame her. How could anyone keep up a home when it could suddenly disappear from beneath you? As far back as he could remember, the family had always been moving, always changing houses. It hadn't been unusual for the family to be forced to move every three months, sometimes even more often. More often than not, they had to move because his father hadn't paid the rent. This was the longest that they had ever stayed in one house since the day Benjamin had been born.

As the houses changed, and the number of children grew, the houses became smellier and dirtier, a place you would never want to bring friends home to if you had any friends. That smell of poverty was stronger than ever in spite of the fact that the family had finally established some semblance of roots.

"Ben!" called Benjamin's mother. "Can you put the coffee on and make some breakfast for the kids? There's some puffed wheat in the pantry. You'll have to make some milk as well. You know where the powder is."

"Yes, Mom."

"Oh, and could you cook up some bacon and eggs for your Dad?"

"Yes, Mom."

Benjamin hated being called Ben, but it was better than Benny which his mother would still use when there was company or when she thought of him fondly as the child he once was. It made him feel like he was a little boy again. He also hated the fact that his father always got to eat well while his brothers and sisters made do with the cheapest meals possible. There was no question that his father was the center of her universe. But, he could never understand why his mother would go out of her way to make it as good as possible for his father as she never knew when his father would be home or even if he was ever going to come back home. Benjamin both hated and loved his errant father.

The children raced down the stairs once they could smell the frying bacon, thinking that somehow, with my return, they were going to be treated to a wonderful breakfast. When they saw the puffed wheat and pitcher of powdered milk sitting on the table beside a stack of stained Melmac bowls, their faces showed their disappointment, at least for a moment. The younger children began asking all kinds of questions as they were asleep when Benjamin had returned to the house.

"Benjamin." shouted Neil, a boy six years old that considered Benjamin as his personal hero. "Where have you been? Are you going to stay? When are you going to start teaching me how to play guitar?" The questions didn't allow any time for Benjamin to give answers. Soon the others began to talk and the kitchen became a noisy place like it always was during breakfast before everyone got ready for school. Without waiting to be asked, Benjamin began to make sandwiches for their school lunches. He knew their favorites and packed their bag lunches accordingly, that is except for Kevin's lunch. Kevin's lunch was just going to be thrown away regardless of what was in it, so Benjamin used the leftover crusts and some orange marmalade for Kevin's sandwiches.

Kevin was always the first out the door, unlike the others, he didn't go to school anymore. He had a job in the city, a laborer's job. As he grabbed his lunch bag, Benjamin slipped him a dollar bill and received a muffled thanks in return. There was only eighteen months difference in their ages and it had been a long time since they had been best friends. Going to different schools once Benjamin started high school had allowed Benjamin to finally begin having friends outside of the house. In spite of the loss of being best friends, they were brothers who had a common enemy, their father. Soon, the honk of a school bus had the rest of the kids who went to school rushing to grab school books and lunch bags.

Benjamin's parents came down the stairs as the kids were leaving. Betsy, his mother, shooed the remaining kids into the living room to watch television while the adults ate. The baby was still upstairs, sleeping. Betsy was only thirty-seven years old her birthday just having passed. Having nine children in less than twenty years had not been kind to her body though her face still managed to hint at the beauty she was as a teenager when she met her husband, Laurent. She stood at five foot one and had auburn hair and gray-blue eyes, a pleasing combination matching her pale skin color. Laurent was dark complexioned with black hair and brown eyes. He was only one year older than Betsy. Though he had put on a lot of weight, he still retained a solid and strong body. He had the striking kind of face that attracted women and the admiration of other men.

"Benjamin," said his father, "I assume you're going to get a job and help out here at home."

"Yes, Dad," Benjamin replied. "I am going to get a job. Don't worry, I will keep helping out like always."

"I knew we could count on you," he continued. "Since you've been gone, we've been having a hard time, what with my hospitalization and not being well enough to work."

It was always the same story, the same constant need. Benjamin had been finding bits of work and giving his mother most of what he earned over the years, even while going to school, always working some small job wherever they lived. The family was poor and as the oldest child, he soon learned that he shared in the responsibility of contributing as much as possible to help meet the needs. He didn't begrudge his mother or his siblings the fact of their need, his anger was directed solely at his father who had repeatedly abandoned them while he chased dreams and other women.

Turning to his mother, Benjamin promised, "Don't worry, Mom, I'll probably find a job today."

"That's nice, Benny," she smiled. "Can you fry up some more eggs for Dad? These are cold, I'll eat these ones."

Chapter Three

Benjamin had been dropped off in the city by his father who claimed to have his own prospects of work that he would be checking out. Benjamin still had about seventeen dollars left from his time in Vancouver. He spend some of that money and bought a book of bus tickets and began searching for work. He checked out a number of grocery stores in which he had worked while in high school. There were no positions available with any of them, however one of the personnel managers suggested that he try a new store in the west end of the city, in the Britannia area. Catching another bus, he made his way to the new store. Once he had filled out the obligatory job application form, he was given a short interview.

It was a relief when they offered him a job even though it only paid minimum wage, a dollar and a quarter an hour. He was to report to work for the night shift and work in the produce section, restocking the counters while the store was closed. He was to begin work that night. He would work six nights a week from nine until six-thirty in the morning, eight hours of pay per night, earning sixty dollars a week with paydays every Friday. It wasn't a lot of money, but it was a job. Somehow he intended to save enough to pay back the money he had borrowed almost two hundred dollars. Because he was to start the job that same day, they asked him to be at the store earlier than normal as they wanted to have him train with the day manager for two hours before beginning his night shift. Of course, they would pay him for those two hours.

It was almost noon and he had a few hours to kill before he had to return to the store and begin working, so Benjamin went downtown. He had more than enough bus tickets until he got paid at the end of the week.

The day was warm and sunny as Benjamin walked along the Sparks Street Mall. It wasn't one of those hot and sultry days that often plagued the city in the summer. Now, as autumn was officially only two weeks away, the weather was as good as it gets. As Benjamin approached the corner he noticed a number of other young guys and their girlfriends who were dressed in bright colored clothes. Long hair, beards, beads, and sandals on their feet, these were flower children. He knew some of them by their first names. They considered Benjamin to be one of them. It wasn't because Benjamin looked like a flower child; it was because he was simply a nice guy and because he was a folk musician.

While two of the guys were playing folk songs by Dylan, Joan Baez and other folk musicians, the girls were dancing and inviting passersby to join them. Benjamin had been playing guitar for six years. For the past three years he had played in his uncle's band on Saturday nights in Legion clubs across the river in Hull and surrounding towns. Benjamin had also been part of a high school rock group that played songs by the Rolling Stones and the Beatles, as well as other British groups that had become popular. Just last year, Benjamin had begun playing folk music and had been able to play in a few coffee houses in Ottawa with other young folk musicians.

Benjamin was tempted to go up to them and talk to them. If he had his guitar, he would have stopped and joined in with adding his music and voice. When he reached the corner of Sparks Street and O'Connor, he hesitated for a moment. Seeing the jewelry shop reminded him of the ring he had bought there for Céline, a black pearl on a simple gold band. It was his promise ring to her. A wave of sadness washed over him for a moment. But as always, he was able to suck it in and bury it deep. With a clearing breath, he finally turned the corner and entered the Canadian Press building to see if friend Derek was in, hoping they could having lunch together.

"Hey, Benny!" called Derek as Benjamin entered the office area where Derek manned the telex machines that were constantly printing out stories that he had to gather and take to the various journalists who worked for C.P. "Where the hell have you been? Jeez, I haven't seen you for almost two months. Where's Céline? At home?"

Punching each other on the shoulder, their way of greeting each other, a guy's way of giving recognition instead of shaking hands or worse still, hugging, Benjamin and Derek re-affirmed their bonds as best friends.

"You know I hate being called Benny, Derek." Benjamin replied. "Céline is in the hospital. Do you want to go out for lunch so that I can tell you all about it?" Benjamin said in response to Derek's questions.

"Yeah, sure. Just give me twenty and I'll meet you, outside. I brought my lunch so get yourself a hot dog or something and buy me a Coke while you're at it," Derek instructed. As the two talked while sitting on one of the benches along Sparks Street, Benjamin told his story about the past two months, mostly talking about the last two days in Vancouver and the events back in Ottawa since his return.

"Your dad's an asshole," Derek stated emphatically. "Hey, check out that chick in the yellow dress. I swear she's not wearing a bra. Probably isn't wearing panties as well," Derek added for distraction talking about one of the young women who was dancing next to the guitar player

"Forget it, Derek. She's Darrell's girlfriend. You remember Darrell, don't you? He's that big guy leaning against the post trying to look cool. You don't want to mess with him, he hurts people. He was in my grade twelve class."

"Still, looking don't hurt nothing. She's hot."

Benjamin had met Derek when they were in grade five, in an English school in Hull just across the river. Benjamin had been the smallest boy in the class and the target of school yard bullies. Derek was taller and unafraid of everyone. However, like Benjamin he was a new kid in the school and isolated because of that. Derek could have easily made friends with the other boys, but there was a rebel streak in him that couldn't be contained, even at the age of ten. He would come to school wearing gray lederhosen, leather shorts with straps over the shoulders rather than the expected gray dress pants that were part of the school uniform for boys. As well, Derek was German, the enemy for the English kids in the school. The school was an English Catholic school in a French city, and the in crowd were all of English descent. Benjamin was French and that was perhaps even worse in the eyes of the in crowd. It wasn't long before they found each other and became friends.

So went the rest of the lunch hour break with Derek flirting with the girls passing by on the street. Benjamin then walked to visit his French grandparents' who lived nearby in an apartment building. Over the past two years he had frequently stayed at their place when it was too late to catch a bus to the southern end of the city from which he had to catch a ride with someone heading towards Carlsbad Springs and the farm house. Benjamin hoped that they would continue to let him stay there when he needed a place to stay in the city.

When his grandmother opened her door and saw Benjamin, she wrapped her arms around him and yelled out to his grandfather, "Gilles! C'est Benjamin!" Giving him a big kiss on the cheek, she asked Benjamin, "Where have you been? Pépère and I have missed you. Did you bring Céline with you?"

Benjamin told his grandmother the sad story while his grandfather sat quietly on one of the kitchen chairs. Gilles was a quiet man, always in the shadow of his wife, Monique. He was of slight build and not a tall man. Benjamin took after him in many ways; his quiet character, looks and his build from Gilles rather than his father, Laurent. Benjamin was their first grandchild and they were inordinately proud of him, thinking him to be the brightest of their more than fifty grandchildren. Monique was short and stout and without question the center of the family's universe. Where Gilles was quiet and serious, Monique was always talking and filled with laughter and spontaneity. She rarely thought before speaking.

"Mon pauvre, Benjamin," Monique consoled. "We were sure that you would marry her. She was such a nice French girl, and that you would have many babies with her." Monique had welcomed Céline into the family when Benjamin first introduced Céline to his grandparents. Gilles simply smiled and nodded at that time, his way of showing his approval of Benjamin's choice. "But maybe this is a good thing," she continued, "Maybe God wants you with another young woman, the right woman."

"Mémère," Benjamin reacted with a bit of a shock. "She is the right woman for me. God had nothing to do with my losing her. It's all because of her mother is a sick woman and can't stand to see Céline finally happy when she's with me."

Benjamin asked his grandparents about again staying at their place, a small apartment on the ground floor of a relatively modern apartment building just a short distance from the Sparks Street Mall. Monique and Gilles had moved there two years earlier when the opportunity to be caretakers of the building came up. Benjamin then told them that he had to begin work in the west end of the city at a large grocery store for the next while until he could find a better job. "I start tonight," Benjamin added, "so I can't stay for supper."

"It's good that you have a job already. Your mother needs the money to help feed your brothers and sisters. It hasn't been easy since Laurent, got sick and lost his job." Monique believed unquestionably in the role that children should play, of giving back to their parents. It was all about the family and never about the individual. At least for everyone but her golden boy, Laurent. Laurent was Monique's favorite child, a fact not lost on her other eight children, a few of whom resented that special status. However, like their mother, most fell under the spell of Laurent being the shining star of the family. "You're a good boy, Benjamin."

Promising to return in the morning after his work shift, Benjamin left the few things that he had taken to the city with him, putting them inside the closet by the door, and then left to make the long bus ride to the store, a journey that took two different buses and more than an hour to complete. Once at the store, Benjamin met with the day produce department manager who gave Benjamin a quick tour of storage and work areas that would be Benjamin's focus during the night shift. When he saw the size of the produce area, he began to understand why they needed two people to work that section at nights when the store was closed.

The manager then asked Benjamin to demonstrate his skills of packaging trays of fruit and vegetables. Benjamin was familiar with selecting product, placing them on cardboard trays and wrapping them with plastic which was then sealed on a heat pad. Satisfied with the results, the manager gave Benjamin the opportunity to grab a quick meal in the staff room before the night manager arrived and the real work would begin.

The store was open every evening until eight with the exception of Saturdays when it closed at six. Though

Benjamin's shift wasn't to start until nine, he was required to be there at least a half hour earlier. As the time for his shift drew near, the night produce manager, Tim, arrived and was introduced. Tim was a young man in his mid-twenties as far as Benjamin could tell. He was slightly overweight, and of Irish heritage. His red hair and beard made him look like someone who worked in the bush, a lumberjack, rather than a produce manager in a big city. Benjamin was relieved that his boss appeared to be a nice guy and not some old geezer who was always angry with the world.

The work was for the most part easy. There weren't very many people working on the night shift, three people who worked in receiving and who stocked shelves when not unloading the various trucks that brought in supplies for the store. Benjamin and Tim had to unload the produce truck that came in every morning around five, as part of their duties. Tim had been working at the store since its opening about five months ago. The guy Benjamin was replacing had quit more than a week ago, an event that meant Tim had struggled to get everything done without help while waiting for someone to take the place of that guy. Since Benjamin had produce department experience, Tim was relieved and soon decided that Benjamin was his next best friend.

By two-thirty in the morning, they had done most of the work needed and decided it was time for a lunch break. Tim suggested that Benjamin could take a short nap in the back room for a while once they had eaten. Tim would wake Benjamin who would then go through the display cases in order to cull spoiled produce. While he was doing that, Tim would take a short half-hour rest. Then, they would clean up the receiving area and coolers in preparation for the day shift's arrival. Benjamin began to think that the job was worth the long travel in spite of the poor wages.

Chapter Four

With work done, Benjamin arrived at his grandparents. It was early enough that they hadn't yet eaten so Benjamin had breakfast with them, hot oatmeal with a liberal helping of brown sugar and real milk. While eating, he told them about the store, about how big it was and that he had a good person to work with during the night. Having eaten, he decided that it would be a good idea if he went home to sleep while the kids were at school. Thanking his grandparents for breakfast he promised to be back in a few days and then left to return home. Taking the bus as far as the Alta Vista shopping center, he then hitched hiked needing two different rides in order to make it most of the way home, leaving him a short walk to the acreage.

The house was quiet with only the TV playing with the volume turned low. Four-year old Justin was sitting in front of it as Benjamin entered the house. The dining room and living room had clothing and toys scattered, everywhere. A large pile of dirty clothing sat near the entrance to the basement where the washing machine was located. The smell of urine was strong telling him that the diaper pail was filled with soiled diapers. Approaching the diaper filled with diapers that hadn't been rinsed, he could smell the shit. He walked up the stairs knowing that his mother would be in her room. He called out as he walked up the stairs hoping that she would answer. The only sound was a burbling by the baby, Heather who was just over a year old, too old to be in the crib that was her bed, but too young to be in a bunk bed with the other kids.

The door to his parents' bedroom was open. His mother was still in bed, sleeping. Heather smiled and raised her hands hoping that Benjamin would let her out of the big steel-framed crib. She was smeared with shit which had escaped out one side of her diaper. The shit was ground into the bed covers as well. Lifting her out of the crib, Benjamin took her to the bathroom and gave her a bath before taking her down to have a late breakfast. Justin came into the kitchen asking for some more breakfast when he heard Heather. The milk from the morning was still on the table along with all of the used bowls and plastic glasses. The bag of puffed wheat was almost empty. Benjamin searched to see what else he could give to his littlest brother and sister. A loaf and a half of bread was all that he found, so he made them some toast which he then covered with a thin syrup he made using tea and brown sugar, a poor man's maple syrup.

While the two ate, Benjamin cleaned off the table and began to fill the sink with water so that the dishes would be washed and ready for when his other brothers and sisters returned home from school. Benjamin was tired and thought of laying on the sofa for a rest. He couldn't take the chance of leaving them unsupervised. As he was finishing with the dishes he heard his mother moan. She had woken up.

"Benny? Is that you?" she called out in a weak voice.

"Yes, Mom."

The only response was more moaning from upstairs.

"I'll bring you some tea when I'm finished taking care of Heather and Justin. Okay?"

Her voice suggested that she was suffering great pain, as if she was almost at death's door. "Okay."

Cleaning a spot off the dining room table, Benjamin got out some broken crayons and unused sheets of three-holed paper from an old binder in his room and set them there for the kids, hoping that they would stay there long enough for him to take some toast and tea up to his mother.

"Here, Mom."

With a groan, Betsy turned onto her back, grimacing as if wracked with unbearable pain. "Can you get me an aspirin?"

Though the bottle was on the end table next to the bed, she waited for Benjamin to open the bottle and take out two small, white pills.

"Where's Dad?" he asked her as she swallowed the pills with a sip of the tea.

"Can you take care of the baby for me? I don't feel well," was her answer.

Benjamin knew it would be wasted effort to try and get any answers when his mother was in one of these states. If he said 'No' he knew his brothers and sisters would have to fend for themselves anyways and that he would be blamed for being an ungrateful, self-centered little prick. It was easiest to just say 'Yes' and let the mood go away on its own. "Yes, Mom."

He left her and went back downstairs. Justin was drawing and Heather was sitting in front of the TV. With both of them occupied, Benjamin sorted the clothing into a number of piles for washing, took down the first load, then returned to the kitchen to finish cleaning it up. He made Heather and Justin bowls of warm milk and cubed bread with white sugar sprinkled on top for a mid-morning snack. He then let them watch some more TV while he rinsed out the shit-filled diapers so that they could be washed. Benjamin thought of the mess in the crib upstairs that needed to be taken care of, but he wasn't ready to go into the room and have to deal with his mother.

With several loads of washing completed, Benjamin took

Justin and Heather outside so that they could play on the grass while he hung out the clothes. While waiting for another load to finish in the washing machine, he played a game with the kids and soon had them laughing. Their laughter brought him a moment of joy as well. It was almost as if they were his children.

It was time to make some lunch for Justin and Heather so Benjamin took them back inside the house. His mother was in the kitchen, sitting at the table with a cup of tea, looking haggard and old in spite of only being 37 years old. Benjamin couldn't remember his mother ever being a well person. She was always sick or on the verge of being sick. The only time she truly smiled was when his father was at home and paying attention to her; or when extended family would come over for a meal and visit. Then, mysteriously, she would revive, make herself look young and beautiful and be the life of the gathering. But always, afterwards, she would slip into a deep state of pain as though the effort to be a great hostess had used up what little reserves she had. And usually, almost always in the last number of years, it was Benjamin's duty to take care of her, to give her some relief.

"Benny," she began, speaking as if she were still at death's door, "Can you clean up Heather's crib? I don't know why she made such a mess. I know I changed her diaper after I sent the others off to school. I think she sometimes does it on purpose just to try my patience."

Benjamin knew his mother hadn't changed Heather since she was put to bed the night before, the traces of shit on the crib were already crusting. He was even sure that it was Béatrice who had changed the baby and put her to bed the night before. His mother had little to do with her children as possible. Finding anger growing within him, Benjamin soon found himself swallowing that anger, something he had learned more than a half lifetime ago. His mother would only take it out on the other children as well as him if he gave in to anger, even if it was justified.

"Yes, Mom. I'll clean it up."

"Can you help me back up the stairs? I don't know if I have the energy to make it on my own."

"Yes, Mom."

"Can you make sure the kids get supper? I just don't feel well enough to do it, today."

"Sorry, Mom," I apologized, "I have to go to work."

Hearing the news that Benjamin had a job, Betsy perked up and asked Benjamin about the job, about how much he would be paid, already calculating just how much of that money would fall into her hands. Benjamin had always turned over most of his earnings to her; sometimes it was the only extra money, outside of welfare, that she had access to. Benjamin told her that he would give her thirty-five dollars every payday and that he needed the rest of his pay to buy bus fare and some clothes for the coming winter. As usual, she complained that it just wasn't enough, that it would mean there would be no Christmas gifts for the children.

It was a skill she honed over the years, to place the guilt on her older children to be the caretakers of the family, to take her responsibility without her authority. And again as it had in the past, it worked. Benjamin began to wonder how he could do with less. He berated himself for being so selfish when he had his brothers and sisters depending on him. He couldn't bear to think that Heather, Justin, Neil, Suzanne and Gordon would be without Christmas gifts. Georges and Béatrice were old enough to earn their own money by baby-sitting, raking leaves, shoveling snow and whatever in order to get some money for gift- giving. Kevin already had a job but for some reason was unable to help much. But, no matter how he tried, he couldn't think of a way to help more. Perhaps if he got the job at Canadian Press he could give her more. Even as he thought of that possibility, he knew that even if he doubled the amount, it would never be enough.

"Will you be home tomorrow? Could you bring some bread and maybe some macaroni home with you?

"No, Mom, I've got a meeting to go to tomorrow. I'm hoping to get a better job."

Betsy's smile returned as she already began to count on getting even more from her first born. "That's okay. We'll manage somehow. Now, help me up the stairs like a good boy."

Chapter Five

"We should go out for a beer and celebrate," Derek said as he slapped Benjamin on the shoulder in congratulations of his first night on the job. "We need to party, man!"

"I'm not old enough to go out for a beer," returned Benjamin grinning at his good luck. "I 'm so glad they hired me. I need to save enough money to go back to Vancouver before Christmas. I can't stand it anymore at home."

"Hey, you remember the day we skipped school and went to a store? You stole a cheap little printing set and I stole . . . shit, I don't remember what I stole, but I remember you said then that you were going to be a writer, a famous writer."

Five weeks into grade five, Benjamin and Derek had skipped classes one afternoon after Benjamin had been beat up and given a bloody nose during the noon hour break. Derek had taken Benjamin to his house to clean up. He told Benjamin that his mother could get the blood off the pink shirt which was part of the school uniform. Rather than return to school, the boys had wandered downtown.

"You stole some dice and a rubber snake," recollected Benjamin.

"I didn't steal the printing set. I paid for it with a quarter I had in my pocket while you were practicing your skills as a kleptomaniac."

"Yeah, that's right, dice and a rubber snake," grinned Derek. "You always were such a goody two-shoes; still are in fact. But what the hell, it takes all kinds."

"Do you remember trying on my lederhosen that day?"

continued Derek. "God, I can still see you standing there in my room with your tiny prick. You weren't even wearing underwear."

"You're a prick, you loser," laughed Benjamin.

Since it was Derek's lunch hour, they both decided that they deserved to treat themselves to some of the famous Nate's Smoked Meat sandwiches and fries.

Walking to the end of Sparks Street, they passed a young man playing a guitar at the corner, Benjamin looked at the guitar, a Martin. He dreamed of one day being able to buy a classic guitar. It wasn't as though his cheap, six-stringed guitar wasn't good, it just wasn't as good. His guitar, a few records and books were all that remained of the things had bought during the year he worked for the Federal Government. His mother had been furious the day he brought home the guitar. He still remembered how her mouth had tightened as though pinched, her dark and threatening stare that burned, and her vicious words about his selfishness. He had paid for the guitar a portion at a time while it sat in the store until it was paid in full. The money he had given his mother had been a windfall in comparison to the small amounts he earned with part-time and summer work while in high school.

Shaking his head of the dark thoughts as they turned and walked into Nate's, Benjamin told Derek that he was starved.

Benjamin left earlier to go to the grocery store. He intended on seeing the main produce manager and giving him thanks for the job. Once at the grocery store later in the afternoon, Benjamin let the manager know that he liked working at the store and that Tim was a great person to work with and for. The manager was pleased at hearing the news especially given Tim's appraisal Benjamin's work.

Hearing this, Benjamin spent the rest of his free time talking to the day staff and helping out where he could. Perhaps he would eventually be asked to work the day shift. Benjamin like the night shift with only one regret that it meant he couldn't take part in the folk music jam sessions at Le Bistro. He just had to think about his reason for working, his intention to return to Vancouver and begin a new life, and the sacrifice was accepted.

With his final paycheck in November in his hand, on his last shift of work for the week as he finally had a weekend off, Benjamin began to doubt the wisdom of giving his two-week notice to the manager as he liked his job at the store. Tim had been allowing him to take home the produce that was starting to spoil; potatoes that were just beginning to show rot as well as some corn that had a few rotten kernels. Tim had also brought Benjamin some things that had to be taken from the shelves because of torn packaging.

Benjamin had been taking this windfall of groceries home for his brothers and sisters. In spite of that windfall, even that wasn't good enough for his mother. For the past few weeks, she had been trying to get Benjamin to bring home a bit extra from the store telling Benjamin that they would never miss a few things that he could take off the shelves, after all, no one would see him take them during the late night shift.

Benjamin had noticed that the groceries he had taken home were becoming the biggest part of what was available to his brothers and sisters leaving him to wonder what his mother was doing with the welfare money that was now not being spent on food. At least he knew that the food he brought home was going to his siblings. There was never a guarantee when it came to giving his mother money.

Benjamin told Tim about his quitting in two weeks, something that wasn't really much of a surprise to Tim as Benjamin had talked often about returning to B.C. to live and work. Tim took a quart of chocolate milk off the cooler shelf and legitimately recorded it in the culled produce ledger as being out of date. Opening the waxed-paper container, he poured a glass for himself and for Benjamin as they sat at a table in the staff room for their midnight lunch break. Earlier between the two of them, they had culled enough potatoes, corn, tomatoes and carrots to make the biggest take-home package yet, for Benjamin.

"I'm going to miss you, Benjamin," stated Tim regretfully. "You're a damn good worker; you know what to do and you're not lazy."

"I've liked working with you too, Tim," he replied. "You've been so good to me and to my family. I don't know how I could ever really thank you enough for all the help you've given me. My brothers and sisters haven't eaten this well in a long time."

"Aw, it's nothing." Dismissed Tim. "It was just going to go into the garbage anyways."

"Still, you didn't have to give any of it to me to take home. I won't ever forget your kindness."

Tim reached out a hand and Benjamin reached out to shake it only to be drawn into a comforting bear hug. "I won't forget you either, Benjamin," he said as he continued to hug Benjamin. The hug seemed to last a bit uncomfortably too long; and when Benjamin felt Tim's hand on his back drop to grasp his behind, Benjamin began to stiffen with realization that Tim had already decided on how Benjamin should thank him.

'Oh, shit!' thought Benjamin in a panic. 'Not again, please God, not again.' He grabbed Tim's arms and whimpered, "Stop! Please stop, Tim."

Tim quickly released his hold on Benjamin's butt as if it was a hot coal. "I thought," he mumbled in an apology, "I thought that you were like me, gay. I'm sorry, Benjamin. When you said you wanted to really thank me, I thought . . ."

"I'm not a homo, Tim," Benjamin apologized. "I don't know why everyone thinks I'm a faggot, sorry, I mean homosexual. It's not like I flirt with guys or that I dream about guys, I don't. I'm only attracted to girls."

The rest of the shift was quiet with little said between Tim and Benjamin and with as much physical distance as possible while the got all ready for the day shift.. Finally, as Benjamin gathered his two bags of discarded vegetables, Tim handed him a gift, a five dollar bill.

"This is for you, Benjamin. I want you to spend it on yourself and not give it to your mother. You're a great guy. I hope that we can remain friends. I'm sorry, truly sorry that I misjudged and touched you. Can you forgive me and be my friend?"

Benjamin's eyes betrayed his surprise. He had thought that Tim was angry with him, believing that he had led Tim on. Five dollars!

"You still want to be friends with me?" expressed Benjamin with a hint of disbelief.

"Why wouldn't I want to be friends with you?" countered Tim.

"I don't know what to say?" responded Benjamin. "Thank you, thank you."

Tim embraced Benjamin in another bear hug, this time a safe hug, and said, "See you, Benjamin, hopefully soon," and then gave Benjamin a light kiss on each cheek before breaking off the bear hug.

Picking up his two bags, Benjamin repeated, "Thanks, Tim, I'm not going to forget your kindness. You're a good guy," as a few tears formed at the edges of his eyes. And then, turning, he rushed out the door hoping that he hadn't missed his bus.

Benjamin had been lucky with the bus connections. He was standing on Hunt Club Road with the bags at his feet with his thumb extended hoping that someone would soon stop as it was cold out. With his luck holding strong, the first passing half ton truck stopped. It was a familiar truck driven by the farmer who lived across the road from the acreage. His name was Mr. Adams. He was a portly and jovial man who liked kids, unlike most of their other neighbors who rued the day when Benjamin's parents moved their nine children into the scattered rural community.

"Whatcha got there, Sport?" he asked Benjamin as he put the bags inside the truck box, tucked behind some boxes so that they wouldn't fall down and spill all the contents.

"Some groceries for Mom," replied Benjamin with a smile.

"I haven't seen you all summer. How come? I never see you jogging down the road anymore."

"I was away in B.C. for the summer, Sir."

"None of that 'Sir' horseshit, Sport. Were you visiting relatives there?"

"Yeah. Mom's brother and his wife live in Vancouver and I stayed with them for a while as I checked out the city. You know, sort of checking it out for possible work there."

"I thought you were one of those 'silly' servants in the city? Didn't you work for the government? I think I remember something about maps or something like that."

"Yeah, I was a civil servant, but it was so boring and the pay wasn't very good. I want to get a real job and make real money, Mr. Adams."

"That makes two of us," he laughed. "There sure as hell is no real money in farming."

Arriving at the entrance to the yard, Benjamin thanked the farmer, gathered his bags from the back of the truck, thanked him again, and then walked down the lane to the house. He had made it home before the kids had left for school. With some apples in the bag, Benjamin was looking forward to giving them each an apple to put into their lunch bags. With this thought in mind, he noticed the old white Ford Falcon sitting next to the house. His father was home. Suddenly all the good feelings vanished.

Seeing the car raised another bitter memory from his final high school year. Benjamin had bought the car for two hundred dollars on down payments, well except for the last twenty dollars, the last payment. He had to leave the car with the seller, a small used car dealer, until the car was paid for in full. While he was in classes near the end of the school year, his father had gone to the car dealer and given him the remaining twenty dollars that was owing and had the bill of sale made out into his name. It was one of the only time that his father had cheated him. His father had lost his last car, a new Tornado, because he couldn't make his payments. Finding out about Benjamin's purchase, Laurent took advantage of the almost free car, a car that wouldn't be repossessed like most of the previous cars he had owned. What made the whole thing such a bitter memory for Benjamin was the fact that his father had never apologized or even expressed thanks. It hadn't been long before his father even forgot that Benjamin had paid for the car.

"Benny's here!" Suzanne called out as he entered the house.

The kids gathered and soon were checking out the bags. Smiling, Benjamin gave them each an apple. There were also two oranges in one of the bags, these he kept aside for his mother who loved oranges. It was only a few moments later that the honk from the school bus had the kids racing for their books, grabbing their paper bag lunches and heading out the door.

Heather was already downstairs, still sitting in her high chair at the side of the table. Justin was munching on his toast covered with strawberry jam, the large jam tin was sitting beside him with jam in clumps on the table and on Justin's clothing. It was obvious that he had put the jam on the toast by himself. Without thinking about it, Benjamin began cleaning up the breakfast mess. As he was running the water in the sink in order to do the dishes, his mother came down the stairs with his father close behind.

"Look, Laurent," Betsy exclaimed. "I told you that Benjamin would bring home some more groceries."

"Hi Mom, Dad," Benjamin mumbled as he turned back to the dishes.

"Benny, be a dear and put on the kettle so Dad can have some coffee?" instructed his mother.

"Yes, Mom."

"Morning, Benjamin," remarked Laurent as he walked by going into the dining room.

"And some tea for me, as well," as she went into the dining room to sit at the table with her husband

"Yes, Mom."

Bringing the instant coffee, a tea bag and two cups with saucers into the dining room.

"Get the tin of Carnation milk for me, Benny," his mother requested. "And the sugar cubes, okay?"

Turning back to get the milk and sugar for her, he answered, "Yes, Mom."

"Did you get paid?" Betsy asked as Benjamin handed her the Carnation milk and box of sugar cubes.

"No, they are going to pay me on Monday night," Benjamin lied. He hadn't told anyone of his plans to leave for Vancouver not long after Kevin's birthday.

Turning to Laurent, Betsy began to apologize, "Sorry, Laurent. I was sure he was getting paid. He's supposed to get paid on Friday's"

Benjamin realized now why his father had spent the night at the house. He was in search of money.

"Benny?" his mother asked in her little girl voice, "Don't you have some money for Dad? He needs some gas money. He has a job interview in Orleans later today and there isn't enough gas in the car to get there and back."

Benjamin knew that the only way to avoid a scene that would

only end up with his father yelling at both him and his mother, was to come up with some money. He thought of the five dollar bill Tim had given him a few hours earlier and then reached into his pocket and pulled it out. Almost as soon as it was out, she plucked it from his hand and gave it to Laurent.

"Here, Love. I'm sorry that's all I can give you. I'll have more soon. I hope it's enough."

With a smile and a kiss, he thanked her, "Thanks, Betsy. I bet the little faggot has the rest of the money stashed away." Then, without staying to drink the full cup of coffee, Laurent walked out the door.

With tears in her eyes, Betsy turned on her son and shrieked, "See what you've done! You made him angry and sent him away." Then, she slapped Benjamin across the cheek and ran up the stairs leaving both Heather and Justin crying, upset with the scene that had just played out in front of them. Justin was still calling out, "Daddy, Daddy, don't leave me."

Benjamin looked at the two crying children and knew he couldn't just walk out the door and disappear as much as he wanted to. Shifting into an unconscious response, he buried it all and then cleaned up both of the kids then took them to sit beside him in the living room, holding them close until they calmed down. It wasn't too long before they began to focus on the cartoons on the TV. Staying with them as they snuggled close to him, he was at a loss to understand how bringing home extra groceries, giving his Dad five dollars for gas in a car that he had paid for, had somehow translated into him being an ungrateful faggot. It seemed the more he gave, the more resentful his parents became. But what worried him the most was what would happen to his brothers and sisters if he left. During the six weeks he was gone, things at home had gotten a lot worse. Seeing that the two had calmed down,

Benjamin went back into the kitchen to finish cleaning up, before he got into more trouble with his mother.

"Benjamin, bring me a cup of hot tea," commanded his mother from upstairs with a tone that said her anger had not abated.

"Yes, Mom."

"You'd better hope that your Dad comes back," she added with more than a hint of a threat as Benjamin gave her the tea." She was back in her bed. The smell of sex permeated the room, a sticky, musky smell that he tried hard to ignore. "Where is the rest of your pay? Why are you hiding it?

"I didn't get paid. I told you the truth."

"You have to have more money. I know that you always hold back some money."

"Mom, I have to have some money for bus fare if I'm to go to work. You know that."

"Give me the money, Benjamin. Now!"

"But what about bus fare?"

"You'll just have to leave earlier and walk. I need the money. Now!"

"Okay," he conceded. Taking out his thin wallet which had another five dollars in it, but not his pay, his mother snatched the wallet and took out all of the five dollars leaving only the last three bus tickets.

"You lying little bastard! You already have bus tickets." She then threw the wallet into his face as she ordered him downstairs to clean up the house in case his father decided to come home after his interview.

By the time the kids got off the bus, Benjamin had made a pot full of spaghetti sauce for their supper. He had also made a few peanut butter and jam sandwiches for their after-school snack and a pitcher of chocolate milk using powdered milk and chocolate milk powder which he had brought home from the grocery store. The chocolate milk powder's container was dented and had a small hole in it, the reason why it was removed from the shelf in the store. For the kids, this was a rare treat.

As they sat around the table, telling their stories of the day spent at school, Benjamin couldn't help but feel better even though there wasn't going to be many more days with them. The only one missing was Kevin who wasn't going to be coming home after he finished work. He rarely came home. Hearing the hubbub, Betsy came down the stairs giving them all a smile. Seeing the chocolate milk on the table and knowing that Benjamin had made some spaghetti sauce, she was quick to take credit.

"I hope you like the chocolate milk that I had Benny bring home for you. And for supper," she continued, "your favorite, spaghetti."

The younger ones were quick to thank her, but the older children focused on the sandwiches as they knew that it wasn't their mother who was responsible for the chocolate milk or the supper on the stove. They had learned the hard way that when Benjamin wasn't home, meals were boring and at many times even missing. Since Benjamin had returned, they had clean clothes to wear to school and they had been able to eat more than just puffed wheat and macaroni.

"Okay, now," she commanded, "Outside and play until I finish making supper. Béatrice, you stay here and take care of the baby." With the orders given, Betsy went into the living room in order to watch her favorite afternoon programs.

"Benny, honey," she called out as she settled herself into her chair, "Bring me some tea, okay? And maybe a couple of cookies if there are any left."

"Yes, Mom," answered Benjamin

"You might want to put the water for the spaghetti on to boil for me at the same time."

"Yes, Mom."

When the supper meal was over that evening, Benjamin got his guitar out and played a few of his brothers and sisters' favorite songs, songs such as; You Are My Sunshine, The Rooster Song, The Gypsy Rover and En Roulant Ma Boule. As he played the songs, everyone sang along whether they knew the words or not. When he played The Rooster Song, he had Neil strum the strings while he placed his fingers on the chords for the song.

Benjamin was Neil's godfather. Neil had been born in a small town in Alberta where their father had a job as town cop six years earlier. With no nearby extended family, Benjamin had been chosen for the role. Benjamin was certain that Neil would be the one who would eventually follow in his footsteps as a musician. The chorus of animal sounds was so enthusiastic, especially when Benjamin changed the last chorus substituting Heather's name for that of the donkey. "I love my Heather, my Heather loves me," began Benjamin. "I cherish my Heather 'neath the green willow tree. My little Heather sings . . ." It was Justin who piped up, "wah, wah, wah," the sound of a baby's crying, that soon everyone was laughing so hard it became impossible to finish singing the song.

Finally, the kids settled down knowing that Benjamin would play for them and sing while they listened. He had learned to play in an Alberta town six years earlier and had worked hard on the music because it helped him cope with life. Even his mother was captured by the songs which were soft and plaintive, songs that allowed his fingers to dance on the fret board where all the pent up emotions found expression and release. Benjamin chose his last song with care, another children's song called Morning Bound Train, which told the kids that it was bedtime.

Chapter Six

The next morning, before anyone was awake, Benjamin took his guitar and backpack with some clothes for the weekend and left. He wasn't going to be coming back until after his next work shift. He intended on staying at his grandparents for the weekend so that he could finally get to go to Le Bistro and hopefully get to play a few songs. He was supposed to meet up with Derek later in the afternoon.

Derek was in a stew because of his father who had once again beaten his mother. This was a story that had been a repeating drama. Derek's father was a successful businessman who drank too much. When tension at work became almost too much to handle, or if his wife Dora complained about his infidelity, Derek's father reacted by taking all of his pent up rage upon Derek's mother; usually verbally, but sometimes crossing the line into physical abuse.

"I swear, someday I'm going to kill the bastard," he fumed.

"Is he worth going to jail for?" Benjamin stated not expecting an answer. "At least he's out of the house staying with his latest girlfriend."

"The slut! She's not much older than I am. He's a fucking moron screwing every female who spreads their legs for him. What the hell do they see in him? He's fat, bald and ugly to boot."

The boys continued walking towards Bank Street passing people finishing up their shopping or, like them, heading to some restaurant for a meal.

Turning the corner, they made their way down Bank Street to a restaurant where they ordered burgers and fries for their supper before heading over to the coffee house in the church basement.

Playing at Le Bistro was something Benjamin loved doing. Since the coffee house was in a church basement, there was no liquor served, just juices, coffee, tea and soft drinks along with a choice of chips and various baked goods. No alcohol meant that those who came were there to actually listen to the music. Eventually the place filled with more people than usual. The two new musicians added to the lineup had brought their own friends along to give them courage and support. Benjamin had the feeling it was going to be a good night.

Benjamin had been given the last set for the evening, the most coveted set by the local musicians, as he had been part of the original group to perform when Le Bistro had opened a year and a half earlier. Once Benjamin's set was finished, the typical conclusion to an evening would be a jam session allowing a few other hopeful musicians in the audience to have an opportunity to be recognized and earn a chance at getting to do a set on another night. While waiting for his turn to play, Benjamin's mood had him sit back quietly in a corner unfocused on the musicians who played. Derek noticed Benjamin's descent into a depression, something he had witnessed so often over the past year and a half since they had reconnected.

"Hey, what's up? Why the silence?" he asked with evident concern.

"I will miss this place when I leave on Monday."

"Don't worry, buddy. You'll find some great places to play in when you're in Vancouver" Derek joked hoping to lighten the mood.

When it was time for his set to begin, Benjamin took the stage and did a last minute check to ensure that the guitar hadn't lost its tune. He set was to last twenty-five minutes enough time to play a number of his favorite songs with one of them being a French folk song which he liked to perform as a bilingual song, adding in a verse in English. Benjamin had been practicing his songs for the past week. However, there was one song that was going through his mind now that he knew he needed to play. He decided to add this song to the list, and play it at the end. He didn't think anyone would really mind since there wasn't another set to follow his.

Years of practice and performing had made Benjamin comfortable on the stage. In spite of all the experience, he always was a bit nervous at the beginning of a performance. Before he would play, he always began by talking to his audience. "It's good to be home," he began. "I want to thank Jeanette and Paul for having me back. This first song, Both Sides Now, is for them."

With that small introduction, he played Joni Mitchell's song slower and in a key friendlier to his voice. He followed the opening song with one by Dylan and then by Simon and Garfunkel, just talking to introduce each song. His second last song was Un Canadien Errant, a song he chose because it felt one that most like his. A song of wandering, loss and homelessness. "This next song is an old French Canadian song that has special meaning for me. For those of you who don't know French, I've put in a verse that tells the tale of the song in English. I hope you enjoy it."

It was time for his last song, he set the guitar aside and began to talk to the audience. "My last song tonight is one I haven't performed before, a song by Simon and Garfunkel. As many of you know, I spent the summer in Vancouver with my girlfriend Céline. Things didn't work out for us there and I came back home because of Céline's health problems. Long story made short, we aren't together anymore. Lately I have been sort of lost. It's almost as if I have found myself wandering aimlessly sort of like the guy in the last song. It's as if I am missing home. I know that most of you sort of feel the same way, unconnected, homeless in spite of going to a place called home each night. But is home a place? I want you to think of that as I sing, Homeward Bound."

Taking a few more moments as the audience sat in silence, Benjamin took a deep breath and then began to sing with more passion and longing that had shown up in any of his songs he had sung earlier. When he was finished, the silence was deafening. Someone coughed and the spell was lifted and applause erupted. It seemed that Benjamin wasn't the only one who felt lost and confused and longing for something lost, something perhaps they had never even had.

"Man," exclaimed Derek. "You were some awesome up there. You were freaking great!"

Benjamin wasn't used to so much positive attention. He knew that he played well and sang half decently, but he also knew that it wasn't his singing or guitar playing that had captured the audience's attention. Unconsciously he had touch a deep longing that was buried in everyone that was there.

After a short break giving everyone time to get a coffee or tea for those that were staying for the jam session, or time to gather up their things and say good-byes as they left, the regulars went up to the stage to begin playing bits and pieces of songs, practicing riffs on their guitars. The newbies were encouraged to join in. Derek had picked up a girl as usual and her girlfriend was hoping that she could catch Benjamin's attention. But, Benjamin's attention was on the music.

A few blocks away, was a Cantonese Chinese restaurant that was the late night place to eat and hang out as everything else in the downtown area was closed. Derek and the two girls were chatting animatedly while Benjamin walked along in silence. When he reached the door to the restaurant, he begged off, saying he was tired and was going to pack it in for the night. Derek shrugged his shoulders, accepting the fact that Benjamin was leaving and said they would hook up the next day before shepherding the two girls into the restaurant for egg rolls and whatever the girls wanted to eat.

Carrying his guitar, music still floating through his head, Benjamin made his way down the dark streets to his grandparents, let himself quietly in. Without turning on the lights, he found a thin blanket with which to cover himself as he lay on the sofa. He lay in the darkness wondering if he would ever find a place he could call home.

Chapter Seven

It was Kevin's birthday, Saturday, December 6th, 1969, Little Christmas. Benjamin had bought Kevin a warm pair of gloves, a tuque and a matching scarf, things that he knew Kevin needed. Benjamin had even given each of his siblings a bit of money so that they could also buy Kevin a little gift. Benjamin knew that being able to give was something that left a good feeling inside, a feeling that for a moment denied the truth of their poverty. Benjamin had been paid the day before, but hadn't yet been home to give his mother the hundred and fifty dollars that had been the agreed upon board and room payment. He had the cash in his pocket intending to give it to her after Kevin's birthday celebrations were over.

Arriving at home in time for supper which had been delayed so that both Kevin and Benjamin could make it there in time, Benjamin was surprised to see his father there. For the last two weeks his father hadn't put in an appearance at the house. Two weeks ago, the last time Benjamin had brought home money. All of a sudden he knew why his father was there. Benjamin wasn't too sure if his father's presence at Kevin's birthday supper was going to be a good thing or a bad thing. His gut told him it wasn't good. When his father was around everyone else became insignificant. Would his father steal the show that belonged on this evening to Kevin? Kevin hadn't arrived yet, which was expected. Benjamin's brothers and sisters were excited as Kevin's birthday meant that Christmas was coming.

Unlike, Benjamin, Kevin had his own car which was just pulling into the driveway. The fact that Kevin had a car and a driver's license and Benjamin didn't was another point of constant criticism from his father. Too many times, Benjamin had heard his father say, "Why can't you be more of a man like your brother?" Though he was always critical and disparaging in his comments to Benjamin about manliness, his father was distant from Kevin. It was confusing, always being negatively contrasted with his younger brother and then seeing his father treat Kevin with what almost seemed like hatred. Benjamin hoped that his father would somehow keep his dislike silent for a change.

Betsy lit the candles on the cake in anticipation of Kevin's entrance. As the door began to open, everyone began singing Happy Birthday. Kevin walked in with a big grin on his face wearing a uniform. He had joined the military. The kids squealed seeing him in a uniform.

"Oh my God!" exclaimed Betsy. "He looks just like my brother Howard!"

Benjamin was the first to give Kevin a hug before standing back, saluting him and then shaking his hand. Kevin was a strong young man in comparison to Benjamin's slight build even though they were both the same height. Kevin had fair hair and skin, obviously taking after his mother's side of the family like Béatrice and Gordon. His mother was right, in a uniform, Kevin looked like his uncle Howard would have looked as a young man. Like a number of his brothers and his sister Béatrice, Kevin had the physical characteristics of the English side of the family.

"You did it!" Benjamin stated with pride as he slapped his younger brother on the back. "You actually did it." Kevin had talked about joining the army ever since Benjamin had returned from Vancouver. When he was younger, Kevin had often talked of being a soldier like his dad.

While the kids made a loud and excited fuss over Kevin, touching his uniform and trying on his cap, Laurent kept silent in the background. Benjamin noticed and was thankful that his father wasn't ruining this special moment for the family. His mother was crying a few tears of obvious joy, another surprise as Kevin had always been her number one target.

"You look so much like your uncle," she repeated as she hugged her second son.

Laurent approached Kevin with his hand extended and a smile on his face. Benjamin smiled in anticipation of seeing his father finally give Kevin his approval. After all, he finally had a son become a military man, following in the footsteps of his father and grandfather.

"Congratulations, Kevin. Your mother is right. You do look like Howard in that uniform. You look like a real soldier. At times like this, I wish that you were my real son, not your mother's bastard. My real son is more of a girl than a man."

Laurent's words were met with a shocked silence.

"Lu!" Betsy cried out, "What are you doing? Please, Lou, not now. It's his birthday."

"Yes, it's your son's birthday. He is a man. Our son is a homo who sucks cocks."

Without thinking about it, Benjamin walked over to his father, "I'm not a homo. And, I sure as hell wished that you weren't my father. How can you find so many ways to screw up our family, to hurt us? Kevin is your son. If anyone is a bastard it's you." And then, he struck out with his fist which his father easily deflected.

Laurent couldn't believe that Benjamin had dared to try and hit him. With a roar, he launched himself at Benjamin and landed two blows that brought blood. Without thinking about it, Kevin came to Benjamin's rescue, pulling Laurent off of him and telling Benjamin to get away, to go to Mémère's and Pépère's and that he would meet him there as soon as he could.

Betsy was screaming and pulling at her husband who then turned around and hit her. While Laurent was distracted by Betsy, Benjamin grabbed a knife and pointed it at his father. The children began scream and cry as they fled the room to hide in their private corners to escape the madness that had descended upon the house.

Threatening his father, Benjamin screamed out, "Get out of our house. Get the hell out and don't ever think of coming back or else I will kill you. You aren't a father, you never were. Get the hell out! Now!"

Laurent reached for his coat and to his wife, "I'll be back, Betsy," he promised thickly. "If he is still here when I come back, then it will be the last time you'll ever see me." The door slammed with the screams and bawling of the kids escalating as the car was started and drove away.

"Mommy," cried Justin, "Is Daddy going to come back? Can you tell him I'll be good, please?"

In spite of the fact that their father had just brutalized the family, each child in the house felt the weight of blame and guilt. If only they had been good enough, perhaps their dad wouldn't have become angry and left.

"Look at what you've done!" screeched Betsy as she slapped Benjamin over and over again. "Get out of my house. Get out! Get out! Get the hell out of my house!" she screamed. Benjamin dropped the knife and covered himself from the blows his mother was raining down on him.

Kevin grabbed Benjamin by the arm and pulled him to the

door. Opening the door, Kevin grinned at his mother and said, "Thanks for the best birthday present ever, Mom," and then laughed as he pulled his older brother through the door and down the steps to the car. Kevin drove Benjamin back into the city. After several minutes of silence Benjamin had to speak.

"What was wrong with Dad? Why did he have to call you a bastard and me a faggot?"

"Because I am a bastard," replied Kevin. "Both Mom and Dad have been telling me for years that Dad wasn't my real father."

"How come I didn't know? Why didn't you tell me?"

"Shit, you had enough problems. If I think I had it bad, and I did, you had it worse, a lot worse. I wouldn't have traded places with you for anything. I don't know how you haven't gone insane or . . ." Kevin didn't finish his thoughts. He knew that suicide had often been something at the edges ready to claim his brother and even himself. Kevin now worried that it was likely close by at this very moment. He had to somehow think of something to keep his brother from committing suicide. "Hell, don't worry about it. We're men now, not boys. We have jobs, careers. He has nothing." Let's go for a coffee and pie, my way of saying thanks for trying to punch Dad and for standing up for me."

They stopped at a Burger King on Bank Street for burgers as both were hungry. Benjamin took a few moments in the washroom to clean off the few blood stains that remained. His lip was beginning to swell from the blow his father had landed. When he returned to the seating area, Kevin had a small crowd around him, almost all of the workers of the burger shop as well as a few customers. The Burger King had been where Kevin had worked for most of the past year. Benjamin had thought that he still was working there before he saw him in a uniform.

"So, when did you enlist?" asked Benjamin when things had settled down.

"About three weeks ago. I quit here last week and have been staying at my girlfriend's place. Her parents are pretty cool, letting me stay in the basement."

"When do you head off to boot camp?" asked Benjamin.

"The day after tomorrow, on Monday. I'm off to New Brunswick. What about you? What're your plans now that you're kicked out of the house? You probably didn't know it, but Mom kicked me out before you came back. I wasn't giving her enough of my pay from this place. While you were gone, I told her to get her husband to give her money, told her that I was done. So, she kicked me out saying I was an ungrateful bastard, of course stressing the bastard part."

"When I would get into trouble stealing stuff or skipping school, Dad would always yell at Mom about my being a bastard," continued Kevin. "Once he yelled at her about sleeping with his brother while he was in Alberta trying to become a cowboy not long after they got married. She yelled back at him about being abandoned with a little baby, that'd be you, about being left alone with a bunch of lunatics that she couldn't understand."

"Yeah, I remember the stories Dad always told about being a cowboy and breaking his arm riding a bucking bronco at the Calgary Stampede," Benjamin said with a shake of his head. "I can't believe that I never knew."

"I thought that you did. I know that Béatrice and Georges knew, and I think Gordon knows as well. I assumed that you had it worse. I got more beatings than you probably because I was always getting in trouble at school, but Mom treated you awful. I was glad that I wasn't you."

"What do you mean?" Benjamin protested, "Mom is always telling me that I was such a good boy, that she could always depend on me."

"Yeah, she'd say that and then she'd . . ." Kevin left his next words unspoken.

"She'd what?" demanded Benjamin.

"Forget it," replied Kevin. "Just forget it."

"She'd what?" repeated Benjamin with an edge of anger. "Damn it, Kevin, finish what you were going to say."

"I saw, so did Béatrice, and sometimes Georges. We saw how she tormented you, how she looked at you with daggers in her eyes. We also saw you do everything she wanted you to do. Everything. She's a perverted witch!"

"That's bullshit and you know it," countered Benjamin with some heat.

"You can deny it as much as you want. But someday you'll have to deal with the truth." The silence weighed heavily and was broken by Kevin who said, "Let's go. I'm sick of this place."

Kevin dropped Benjamin off at their grandparents. It was late enough so Benjamin didn't have to spend time talking about the evening with them. They had already gone to bed as he let himself into the apartment and then sat on the sofa with his head in his hands.

"Benjamin? C'est toi?" called out his grandmother.

"Oui, Mémère, c'est moi." He listened as his grandmother settled down and her snores began to resonate through the small apartment.

He remained sitting on the sofa for most of the night, unable to sleep. His mother had told him to stay away. Did she really mean it? He'd have to phone in the morning, after she had time to cool down. Likely it was just another storm that would soon be forgotten. Benjamin began to talk himself into believing that she would tell him to come home, that it was okay. Benjamin was glad that it was Saturday night as it meant he didn't have to go to work in the morning.

His grandmother woke him with the sounds of her preparing breakfast. "Did you have a good time last night? I thought you were going to stay at home for the rest of the week- end?" his grandmother asked as Benjamin sat at the table joining his grandparents for breakfast.

"Yes," he lied knowing that he couldn't tell the truth about what had happened. Despite everything, they loved his father. "Kevin showed up in his new uniform. He's going to be a soldier."

His grandmother beamed as she repeated the news to her husband, "Gilles, did you hear that? Kevin is going to be a soldier."

For his response, Gilles smiled and nodded before adding, "Just like Laurent and me."

When breakfast was done, Benjamin helped his grandmother with the dishes then did the rounds of the apartment building with his grandfather. Benjamin felt comfortable with his grandfather's quietness. As usual, his grandfather was chewing on a cigar which he had forgotten to light. And, as usual, he was wearing his favorite hat even though they didn't go outside to do the rounds.

With the rounds done with only one light bulb needing replacement, they went back to the apartment for a mid-morning coffee before his grandfather would leave to meet up with some of his old buddies for their usual Saturday morning gathering. When he left, Benjamin made the phone call home. Béatrice answered the phone.

"I don't think she wants to talk to you," she told Benjamin.

"Just ask her," Benjamin asked. A few seconds later, his mother was on the line.

"What?" Benjamin could hear the snarl in her voice over the phone line.

"Is it okay if I come home later today? I have to finish fixing the clothes line in the basement."

"No, you hit your father. Stay away," she screamed and then slammed down the phone.

Benjamin quickly put on his coat and left telling his grandmother he would be back later trying to disguise his panic.

Walking the streets, Benjamin tried to make sense of what had happened, tried to figure out what he was going to do until his mother's temper cooled down. Finally, he stopped at a restaurant to get warm with a cup of coffee. As he sat, slowly sipping the hot coffee, he began to think that maybe his mother wasn't going to change her mind. He began to think about what had been said by his father, his mother and Kevin last night. Benjamin felt lost and had begun to believe that he wouldn't be going home again. With that thought, he became both angry and depressed. No home, no Céline, no point in staying in Ottawa.

Perhaps it was time to leave, to return to Vancouver and start a new life. Benjamin realized that he hadn't given his mother any money the night before. The storm happened so quickly, that his mother hadn't thought to get her money before she threw him out of the house. Benjamin had enough money to pay back his uncle and buy a train ticket. But what about his guitar and his books and stuff? Knowing that whatever was in the house was basically lost, he saw little reason to wait. The sooner he left, the better. But first he had to make a few phone calls beginning with home. He hoped his mother didn't answer the phone.

"Hi, Béatrice?"

"Hi Benjamin. She didn't change her mind. She's madder'n a hornet and she's taking it out on us."

"Just listen for a minute," urged Benjamin. "I leaving Ottawa. You can have my room if you want it."

"Hey, thanks, Benjamin. Of course I want it." Benjamin could almost hear her smile.

"Let me talk to Georges." While waiting for Georges to come on the line, he planned who would get what of his few possessions at home. "Georges, I'm leaving Ottawa. You can have all my clothes if you want them. You're almost the same size as me. Give Gordon my books if he wants them. Suzanne and Neil can have my records. Shit, I don't know what to leave for Justin and Heather. I'll send something later."

"I'll give them something and say it's from you. Don't sweat it, Benjamin." Georges was the only one of his siblings besides Kevin who called him by his real name. "Let me know where you are when you figure it out. It looks as though I'll have to take over from you here. You know Béatrice, she's not strong enough to deal with Mom. Don't worry, it'll work out."

"Thanks Georges. Let me talk to Gordon, Suzanne, Neil and Justin. I have to say good-bye. I love you, Georges. Take care of yourself and the kids, okay?"

"Sure, man. Here's Gordon."

Benjamin spent the next few minutes saying a few words to each of his siblings except for Heather. Of all the kids, Neil was taking it the hardest. It was only when he found out that he was going to have the guitar that he stopped crying. Benjamin had to promise that he would come back and give him some lessons in the future.

Early Monday morning, Benjamin called his best friend. "Derek?" he began.

"Hi Benjamin. What's up?"

"I'm heading to Vancouver."

Derek told Benjamin to wait until later in the afternoon before heading to the train station to buy tickets. He wanted to be there with him. Derek promised to be there in three hours as he had a few things he needed to take care of before he could come to the apartment. Hanging up, Benjamin wondered what he would tell his grandparents. With any luck, they would still be at bingo when he left.

Benjamin just had enough time to go to the bank and withdraw his savings which he added to the money in his wallet. On the radio, back at his grandparents, he listened to the announcer talk of a riot at Altamont, California at a concert calling it "The Day The Music Died," December 6th, 1969

"What's with the bag?" Benjamin asked when Derek showed up. Benjamin's grandparents were still out, but not for much longer. "Before you answer, let's get out of here before I have to start answering questions. As they walked out the door and began walking, Benjamin saw his grandparents driving by and waved to them. "Whew! We left just in time. Now, what's with the bag?"

"Did you think I was going to let you go alone? No goddam way."

"What?" replied Benjamin, too surprised to say anything else.

"I'll tell you all about it on the way to the train station. Hustle your ass, there's the bus."

Part Two

Taking Detours Along The Road

Chapter Seven

The train was moving again following the last stop in Saskatoon. Few people had got off the train at the stop and fewer got on the train. Both Benjamin and Derek were tired after a long day travelling though the bush of Northern Ontario and another part of a day through the open flatlands of Manitoba. They had coach tickets which meant they had to sleep in their seats. When they found out the cost of a sleeper bunk, they decided that it would be better to save as much of their money as possible for Vancouver as they needed something to live on until they got a job and their first pay cheque, and who knew how long that would take.

"She looks pretty hot," Derek commented about one of the new passengers that slipped into a seat not far from theirs.

"They all look hot to you, Derek," remarked Benjamin with little enthusiasm. "Why don't you see if she'll let you be her knight in shining armor while I try to sleep? Maybe you can show her a good time in the dining room car."

"Loser. Maybe she's your type. Did you ever think of that?"

"Do I have a type, Derek? It seems guys are more attracted to me than women. I'm twenty god-damned years old and I'm still a virgin. Doesn't seem that I have a type of woman or that she's one of them."

"Hmm?" wondered Derek, "Maybe you look hot to me, too," he laughed as he punched Benjamin on the shoulder. "I'll be back later and let you know what you missed."

Derek left his seat next to Benjamin and walked through the car and on to the next car. On his return, he stopped to chat with the girl who had gotten on in Saskatoon. It didn't take very long before he was sitting beside her. Benjamin wondered how Derek did it. What was it about Derek that convinced girls and women to drop their panties without protest?

Benjamin thought of all the nights he had slept beside Céline, most of those nights with both of them nude. Not once had he been able to make love with her. She had trusted him she said. She had told him he had a beautiful body and had done several nude sketches of Benjamin during the past summer while she was nude as well. He was allowed to cuddle, to touch her intimately and to kiss all of her, but that was all. Intercourse was not something she could allow.

Sitting alone on the train, Benjamin's thoughts continued to drift back to the first few days of their flight to Vancouver last July. Neither of them had taken extra clothing along. He only had the clothes he was wearing; undershorts, grey tweed slacks, an undershirt and a long-sleeved shirt, along with his guitar. Like him, she only had the grey short skirt, a blouse and her panties for clothing. Her breasts were small and she never wore a bra. She also had her purse and art portfolio. Their flight from Ottawa had definitely not been planned. With that thought, Benjamin had to grin thinking that this present flight from Ottawa wasn't well planned either. True, he had extra clothes, stuff he kept at his grandparent's place, and he had more money now than he had then. His thoughts turned back to that flight to Vancouver.

While Benjamin was reliving the past with Céline, Derek returned unnoticed.

"Hey, buddy," quizzed Derek. "What's on your mind?"

"I was just thinking about last summer and Céline."

"I hope it was all good."

"Yeah," Benjamin confirmed with a sigh and a smile, "It was all good, maybe too good."

They got off the train in Vancouver, each carrying one bag. It was late enough in the day for Benjamin's uncle or aunt to be at home from work, so Benjamin phoned hoping that they would let them stay for a few days until they found their own place. The job hunt was to start this evening with a search through the want ads in the newspaper. The phone was answered on the second ring.

"Hello?"

"Hi, Jennie. It's Benjamin. I'm back in the city."

"Where are you? When did you get back?" she asked with her typical cheery voice. Benjamin liked his aunt better than his uncle. He had been an usher at their wedding four years earlier.

"I'm at the train station. We just got into the city."

"Is Céline with you?" she asked with surprise.

"No, I'm with my friend, Derek. You remember him, the guy who went to Montreal with me when you lived there?"

"Oh yes, I remember," she said. "Why don't you come over for supper? Ben will be home soon. Do you have a place to stay?"

"Not yet," Benjamin admitted. "We were going to check into the YMCA." It was a lie, but Benjamin didn't want his aunt to think he simply assumed using her place as a hostel.

"You can stay here for the night. We'll talk when you get here. You remember where we live, don't you?"

"Yeah. We'll be there in about a half hour I think. Thanks Jennie."

They consulted the transit map and decided on taking a bus to get to the apartment in which Benjamin's aunt and uncle lived. When they got to the apartment, his uncle had already arrived. He opened the door and shook both boys' hands.

"Well, well," he said as they entered the apartment. "Look at what the cat dragged in."

"Hi, Uncle Ben," greeted Benjamin as he returned the handshake. Benjamin never understood why he had to call him uncle as he was only four years older. If it wasn't for Jennie, he would never have turned to his uncle for help last summer. "Here, I have something for you," continued Benjamin as he handed him an envelope.

"Well, well," Ben remarked as he took the proffered envelope. "What do we have here?"

"Open it up and you'll find out," grinned Benjamin in anticipation of his uncle's surprise.

Opening the envelope, Ben saw the money and for a moment was speechless. "Well, well," he finally spoke, "you are probably the only person in the history of your family who's ever paid a debt. I'm surprised. I had figured that it was money thrown out the window. I wasn't even going to give you the money because of your family's reputation. But, Aunt Jennie talked me into it. I'm impressed. Thank you."

The 'thank you' was unexpected, and because of that, feeling appreciated. Benjamin began to warm up to his uncle who was a living model of the British 'stiff upper lip' that was typical of most English Canadians who came from aristocratic, or semi-aristocratic British roots. Jennie was smiling and called everyone to the table for supper. Even though Benjamin had come from a poor family, she had put out her best china, Royal Dolton.

When the meal was over, Benjamin asked if they had a recent newspaper so that they could check the want ads for work.

"You are full of surprises, young Benjamin," exclaimed Ben. "Next you'll be telling me that you are also looking for your own place."

"Of course," Benjamin replied. "Derek and I have no intention on being dependent on anyone. We both have money to get started on our own," he added with a bit of defensiveness.

"Well, well," Ben returned. "But of course you'll stay with us until you find a place. Is that okay with you, Dearie?" he asked expecting no answer. "See, it's all settled. So, tell us about Céline."

By the time Benjamin had finished the barest outline of Céline's current status in Ottawa, leaving out everything about his family and the events that had brought him back, it was late enough to call it a night. Benjamin got to sleep in the same bed he had shared with Céline on his last stay at their place. Derek was given the couch for his bed. Then, Ben and Jennie retreated to their room for the night.

"He's still a stiff bastard," commented Derek.

"Shh! They'll hear you."

"Not a hope. Can't you hear them going at it in their room," snorted Derek. "He won't be hearing a damn thing until he wakes up in the morning."

"At least we have a place to stay until we get a place of our own," Benjamin reminded him.

"You can stay here. I don't fancy sleeping on his sofa and having to feel as though he has done me a favor. When we get a place and a job, we'll be set. So what did you think of that ad for Auditing Clerks?"

"Sounds like something I could do in my sleep. Numbers are easy for me. And," Benjamin added, "I did work for the Feds for a year punching calculator keys. What do you think?" Benjamin asked.

"Sounds to me as if it's worth a try. It sure seems better than the other options in the paper. No damned way that I working in the bush on the side of a mountain."

The next morning, both young men went to the address mentioned in the advertisement where they found themselves as part of a large group applying for the few job openings. Once they had registered and filled in a job application, they were told to wait their turn to take an aptitude test.

Benjamin finished first and handed back the test to the person at the desk who took it almost unwillingly.

"Don't you want to try and finish the test?" she wondered.

"I did finish it, see?" Benjamin said as he showed her the three pages. "All the questions are answered."

Derek was already at the desk waiting to hand his test in as well. They waited as she checked over their tests.

"You two can go and sit in the waiting room behind that door.

I'll call you when it's time for the interviews. There's coffee in there, too. Just help yourselves."

While they waited, about eight others eventually came into the waiting room. Most of them were guys with the exception of three girls. Only five people were going to be hired, so the odds were beginning to look good. Finally, the interviews began. There were three men in suits, the woman who had given them the test and another man in casual clothing who looked as though he needed a drink judging by the look of his face, who comprised the interviewing team. Derek was called in first, then the three other guys before they called one of the girls. Benjamin was beginning to lose hope. What if they were interviewing based on test scores? He was beginning to think that he had messed up somehow. Both remaining girls were assigned the next interview times. Benjamin was sweating with nerves as finally his name was called for an interview.

"So, why did you apply for this job?" asked one of the men in suits.

The question surprised Benjamin. "I need a job. I'm a good worker and I learn fast." Benjamin replied, perhaps a bit too nervously.

"You had the highest score on the test and finished it faster than anyone has ever written the test before," added the woman. "This job isn't that good. We are worried that you'll quit almost as soon as a good job comes around," she continued. "Do you have other job applications out? Where and with whom?" she added assuming a positive answer.

"No, this is the only place I have applied to. My friend and I just got to Vancouver yesterday."

Feeling nervous and thinking that they weren't going to give him one of the positions because they thought he was only just going to quit as soon as he could find a better job, he said "If you give me a chance, I won't even look for another job." In desperation he added, "I'll sign a contract if I have to. I want this job. You won't be disappointed in me if you'd just give me a chance. "

Looking at the others at the table, one of the men in suits said, "Go sit in the front office on one of the chairs. We have to have a little discussion. We'll call you back in to let you know our decision."

Benjamin walked into the front office and found five others sitting there as well, the three girls, Derek and one of the three guys that had also been interviewed. About a minute later, the door opened and the name of the other guy was called. After less than a minute, he walked out looking disappointed. He picked up his jacket and walked out of the office. After a few more minutes the door to the interview room opened and we were all called in as a group.

"Congratulations. We are pleased to welcome you to our team. You are one of three groups that will be working for us, representing our firm in various communities around the province. Your group will be responsible for inventory control for our customers on Vancouver Island. A second group has already been assigned to the lower mainland region, and our third group is taking care of the Vancouver region.

"I want to introduce your boss, Doug. He will be your driver, babysitter and warden. Do what he asks you to do without asking questions. Once this meeting is over, Doug will take you to our warehouse where you will learn how to use a comptometer. You'll return to the warehouse for two more days of training on dates that will be given to you by Doug. Doug will also be giving you employee employment forms for you to fill out, forms which you need to give back to him today before he drives you to your respective lodgings. Any questions?"

Derek was the first to ask a question. "Do we get paid for our training? How much are we going to be paid?" he added.

Looking at each other as though pleased with the questions, the men nodded to Doug who answered, "Yes, you'll be paid for the training sessions. Your salary rates will be on the forms that I will be giving you once we get to the warehouse."

One of the young women asked, "When will we actually begin working?"

Doug answered, "We will be leaving Vancouver on December 30th, I will be picking you up from your homes early that morning. Again, I will letting you know more about that, likely at the last training session. Any more questions?"

The oldest man at the table, the one who had been quiet during the group interview spoke up once no one else offered another question. "I think we're going to have the best team ever ladies and gentlemen". With a smile and his arms extended he continued, "Welcome to the Canadian Inventory Management and Control family.

Doug led the way out of the office with the five new hires following. He stopped to say a few words to the office secretary who then handed him a packet of large envelopes. Turning to the group he said, "Let's go. I have a van just outside the door that will take us to the warehouse."

It wasn't long before Derek began to flirt with the girls who were quick to shut him down. Benjamin had a laugh at Derek being put into his place so quickly, something that didn't happen all that often. The work itself was relatively easy once they had mastered the technique of using most of their fingers to work the keys of the comptometer. Then, it became a matter of building up speed so as to enter data quickly.

Their task was to calculate the number of items on shelves then enter either the cost price or the selling price of these items. They practiced working in teams and working on their own. Since Benjamin was quick with his fingers, likely due to years of finger practice playing a guitar, he could take the data given by two people counting inventory and then shouting out the data to him.

After the day's training session was done, Doug drove them to their homes, offering to take anyone back to the office if they had driven to the interview. As they drove off, Doug told them that he would pick them up at their places the next morning for another day of training at a different location. He also told them that they would be having their last training on Sunday where they would use a real store for a test run. Doug let the girls off first. One was living at home with her parents, one was living in a basement suite, and the third had a room in a house. As Doug drove Benjamin and Derek to Benjamin's uncle's address, Derek agreed to stay with Benjamin until he could find them an apartment of their own.

At the evening meal, Benjamin's aunt told them about a house just two blocks away on the same street which had rooms for rent, a house in which the residents shared the kitchen, dining room, living room and bathrooms. Derek looked at Benjamin and grinned before asking Jennie more about the house. Jennie gave them the contact phone number and suggested they might as well find out more from the person renting out the rooms.

A call to the owner resulted in both boys heading over to the house as soon as the meal was done. Promising to do the dishes when he returned, Benjamin thanked Jennie for her help. Arriving at the house, an older house with a large sunroom in what used to be the front porch, the boys met the owner who gave them a quick tour of the house. He showed them the three bedrooms available, and told them the rental rates. Derek chose one of the two rooms on the upper floor that looked out onto the street and Benjamin chose a smaller room on the ground level that had a private door into the back yard. Derek asked the owner when they could move in. With the response that the rooms were ready and waiting for them and that they could move in whenever they were ready. Agreeing to rent the rooms, the boys put a deposit on the rooms. They would be required to pay a portion of a month's rent for what remained of December, as well as for the rent for the whole of January. Luckily, both had enough to cover the cost though it left very little left.

Returning to Jennie and Ben's with smiles on their faces, they shared the good news.

"Well, well," responded Ben. "Now that was quick. So when are you moving in?"

Derek was the first to answer, "I'll be moving my stuff over there tomorrow. Is it okay if I stay another night?"

"No problem, Derek," laughed Ben. "We won't charge you too much for the extra night." Seeing the surprise on Derek's face, Ben continued, "Of course I'm joking. Jennie and I would love to have you stay as long as you need."

"I'll be taking my stuff over there at the same time," stated Benjamin.

"Oh no, you're not!" Jennie commanded. "You have to stay until at least Boxing Day. You're family and there's no way you're leaving, young man." Turning to Derek, she continued. "And as for you, you haven't any choice but to be here for Christmas and Boxing Day as well. That's settled."

Benjamin laughed and answered. "Yes, Aunt Jennie."

"And none of this Aunt stuff. I'm only three years older than you. You're making me feel as if I'm old and wrinkled." Turning to Ben, she said, "Ben?"

"You don't have to call me Aunt as well," he grinned.

"Ben!" Jennie threatened.

"Ben it is then," countered her husband with a laugh as he clapped Benjamin on the shoulder.

Chapter Eight

It was early morning when Doug picked them up two days before New Year's. He had told his new team that they would be staying on Vancouver Island for the next ten days and that they would be staying at different motels as they travelled to various towns on the Island doing year-end inventories for a number of the company's clients. He also told them that he would be giving them a daily meal allowance each day, in order to take care of meal allowance. Whatever they didn't spend, they could keep. There first job was scheduled for the afternoon in Victoria, a gift shop. There was also a drug store that would be done later that same day which would mean they would be getting to their hotel late. With that information given, Doug turned on the van's radio and drove them to the Tsawwassen ferry terminal.

Almost immediately, the excitement level in the van rose significantly. All five of the new team members were about the same age with Jacqueline who was still seventeen being the youngest and Derek the oldest at twenty-one, the only one in the group who was old enough to legally drink. Derek was untypically quiet. He hadn't returned to the house until well after midnight. Benjamin guessed that he was suffering from a hangover.

They were lucky enough to make it onto the first ferry, but many of the others behind them weren't. The line-up was huge. Once on the ferry, Derek found a group of unoccupied seats and stretched out on them for a nap. Benjamin lined up with the girls and Doug for a coffee and a muffin. Doug had given them their meal allowance for the day just as they left the van once it was parked on the ferry. Benjamin hoped it would be enough for breakfast. Having heard that he got to keep the money not spent on meals, Benjamin was already seeing the meal allowance as a windfall. Not needing to spend his own money on meals would allow him to buy a new guitar sooner that he had hoped for. From the looks of the trays that the girls carried, they appeared to be thinking the same thing. Doug had ignored getting a tray and simply bought himself a large cup of coffee.

The trip took almost two hours. As they neared the dock on Vancouver Island, all five members of the team were standing outside on the deck. Doug had gone down to the parking level to the van and was waiting for them. When the ferry slowed, they decided it was time to join Doug in the van. In less than an hour they would be putting their new skills to work for real. They were nervous and excited at the same time and their laughter reflected it.

"Okay, everyone will work on their own in this store because of the tight quarters," noted Doug as he opened the back for access to the comptometers. "The cost code for this store is 'Blacksmith.' You have to hurry as we want to get to the next place before supper if possible. And remember, if you break something, you pay for it."

The cost code was a ten-letter word in which no letter was repeated, with each letter of the word assigned a number from one to zero for each letter of the word. "Blacksmith" meant that the letter B represented the number 1, the letter L represented the number 2, and so on. Stores used these codes to both tell themselves what they had paid for the various products, and to keep that information secret from their customers. The work progressed slowly for the first hour and began to pick up speed as time wore on and the five began to get into the flow of counting, computing and recording. They stopped for a lunch break and headed out to a nearby Macdonald's fast food outlet. Doug rushed them through their lunch and soon they found themselves back at the gift shop.

With food in their stomachs and growing confidence, they finished doing the store's inventory by mid-afternoon.

Doug congratulated them, "That was great, good work team. Now we are going to a drug store near our hotel, so I will stop there first so that we can drop off our bags. I have booked two rooms for the gals – you'll decide who gets the room alone – and a double for the guys. I will give you your keys once I have checked us in. Take a few minutes in your rooms, no more, to do your business and then hustle back out to the van. Got it?" Getting nods of assent Doug walked to the front desk where he began chatting with the receptionist as though they were familiar friends.

Derek and Benjamin were the first to arrive at the van after having dumped their bags, and going to the toilet. They waited another fifteen minutes before the girls arrived.

"What took you so long?" quizzed Derek, annoyed at having to wait for them. "The sooner we get done, the sooner we're back."

"Don't get your shorts tied into a knot," yelled Betty.

Doug smiled and then drove off to the drug store. "The code for Family Drugs is "Breadstick". You can work in teams in this store. Derek, you work with Betty and Linda; Jacqueline, you team up with Benjamin. The team that records the most items wins a free beer."

Derek and his teammates rushed into action, determined to get the beer. Benjamin and Jacqueline had both agreed that there wasn't any need to compete as neither of them drank. However, it was soon obvious that the friction between Betty and Derek was causing problems.

"Jesus, Derek!" complained Betty, "Give me that thing Mr. All Thumbs." I sure the hell hope that you at least know how to count."

Eventually, they settled down and in the end it was close with Benjamin and Jacqueline barely winning the beer.

"Don't worry," laughed Benjamin. "You can drink mine for me, Derek. I think I'll be satisfied with a Coke tonight, at your expense of course."

Jacqueline followed his example and offered her beer to Betty. Sitting together in the hotel restaurant eating burgers and fries, the tension of the day fell off the five young people. Doug was at a separate table with a few other older people including the clerk who had been at the counter earlier in the afternoon. It was obvious that Doug had been here many times before. Finally, with the food all gone, the five young adults decided it would be good to enjoy a swim and sauna before heading to bed. There first job tomorrow was at seven-thirty. Doug had arranged wake-up calls so that they would have time for a quick hotel breakfast before they left.

The swimming was ditched as most hadn't thought to bring bathing suits. It was a tired group that sat in the sauna with towels wrapped around themselves. The heat of the sauna and the long day of work had reduced them into silence. When Linda announced that she'd had enough and was going to bed, the others were quick to echo their goodnights. As a group, they walked down the hallway wearing their towels to their rooms which were just across from each other. Just before going into the room, Derek called out Betty's name. As she turned, he dropped his towel and mooned her. Everyone, including Betty laughed and then again said 'Good night.'

The second day was busier than their first day, but for some reason, when they gathered at the hotel in the evening, New Year's Eve, there seemed to be a lot more energy than there was the evening before. After they had eaten, Derek had ordered beer for all of them including Doug, and toasted the New Year. Because they were to leave even earlier the next day in order to drive to Parksville where two stores would be inventoried, there weren't any plans to go out on the town later that evening for New Year's Eve. Betty took her turn and ordered a second round of beer.

Benjamin wasn't able to finish his glass of draft by the time the group had decided to give the sauna a second go. Derek, Linda and Betty took a third glass of beer with them to their rooms. The doors to their rooms were left open while they stripped off their clothes and wrapped towels around themselves. Derek and Benjamin crossed the hall and entered the girls' room where the girls were opening cans of beer while laughing. Caught up in the revelry, Benjamin took a can and drank from it. It was a good twenty minutes later, just after eleven when they noisily went down the hallway to the sauna.

The heat and reduced inhibitions thanks to alcohol had them drop their towels as they flopped onto the cedar benches, sweating. There was no sense of their nudity being anything other than innocent relief. It was Jacqueline who brought up the idea of cooling off in the pool. The heat and the beer had left them more than a little tipsy as they tried to cover themselves again with towels before exiting the sauna. With a whoop, Derek jumped into the pool only to have his towel fall off as he hit the water. Jacqueline was in the water with her towel still in place as the other two girls struggled to enter the pool with their towels. Benjamin stood looking at the group deciding if he would enter into the pool when Jacqueline got out of the pool, pulled away his towel and pushed him into the water. Then, demurely, she dropped her own towel and dived in after him.

The noise of their partying in the pool had attracted the attention of a private New Year's Eve party that was taking place in the convention room next to the pool. When the door opened giving the party goers a view of the five young people, naked in the pool, several of the male guests decided to jump into the pool with their suits on. The raised noise level soon brought in hotel staff who demanded that all get out of the pool as it was closed. Strangely, no one protested. Wrapping wet towels around themselves, the five returned to their rooms where they then threw the towels into a tub. Sitting on the beds and on the floor along the wall, the toasted the New Year with a final can of beer. As if by agreement though nothing was said, there was no exchange of New Year's kisses. Laughing as they left Linda and Betty's room, the boys and Jacqueline separated into their separate rooms and called it a night.

"That was some New Year's Eve party you guys had last night," Doug commented with a chuckle as they drove up the Malahat towards Parksville. "It's a good thing we are at a different motel tonight."

Still wearing big smiles, they all agreed with Doug's statement.

"Did you see that blond chick in the green dress push that guy in, you know the one who was pretending to be disgusted while ogling Betty's boobs?" Linda asked.

"Well, Betty, you do have big boobs," Derek confirmed. "I know from firsthand experience. I had more than one good look last night."

"You're a pig," Betty complained. "At least they're not little like those peanuts you have for balls."

"Ouch!" Jacqueline quipped. "She got you there, Derek. Your balls are small, like your dick. Now, Benjamin's, well that's more what I'd expect a real man should look like."

"Bullshit!" rebutted Derek. "Who are you to make statements about a real man? Not much in the way of boobs in your case, is there?"

The bantering continued all the way to Parksville. Just as they entered the small city, Doug told them the keyword for the inventory, "Backslider", which had them all laughing as they caught an unintended sexual connotation to the word.

The day passed quickly and they were able to eat an earlier supper than usual. Doug had recommended the clam chowder which they all decided was worth a try.

After a few mouthfuls, Benjamin pushed his bowl away and ordered a plate of fries. "Ugh. Well that was a waste of good money," he muttered.

"Pass it over here if you're not going to eat it," said Derek. "You're right, Doug, this clam chowder is delicious!"

After the meal, Benjamin and Derek went for a walk along the shoreline next to the motel.

"I like the work and the girls," Benjamin began. "I haven't had so much fun in a long time."

"I told you beer was good for your health," laughed Derek. "It makes the world a better place, a lot more fun as well," he added. "Yeah, it's pretty cool. I see that Jacqueline has the hots for you"

"Naw, she's got a boyfriend in Vancouver. She was telling me that he lives with her in her basement suite. Besides, I'm not interested in having a girlfriend, yet. I just want to work, earn enough money to buy some nice clothes and get myself a new guitar."

"Same here," admitted Derek. "Except for the guitar part," he added with a laugh. "Let's head back and see what the girls are up to."

Like their hotel in Victoria, the motel had a sauna into which the five soon found themselves. Only Benjamin and Linda had bothered with towels. After a bit of friendly teasing, the towels were set aside and used to wipe the sweat off faces. It seemed strange to Benjamin how non-sexual it was, being naked together in the sauna. Even Derek had left off talking about sex. Benjamin's worries about getting an erection and having everyone see it and laugh at it, soon vanished. It wasn't as if they didn't see each other's privates, or that they were deliberately trying to avoid looking. Rather, they were seeing each other naked and accepting that their nakedness was natural and that each of them were much more than nude bodies, more than exposed skin. Curiously, they began to see each other beneath their skin, to see themselves as they really were.

As they sat there in the heat with the conversation fading into silence, they disappeared into their own inner worlds. It was a tired group that made their way to their rooms for the night.

Doug started the van as the group climbed in. The ferry had docked and the gate had opened with cars and trucks already beginning to leave the ferry. It had been a long stretch away from Vancouver. Benjamin had managed to save enough from eating as cheap as possible and avoiding stupid expenses such as smoking and beer. After the New Year's Eve adventures, he had steered clear of taking another drink. He didn't do well with hangovers. Derek managed to save only a few dollars over the ten days due to his need for alcohol. Benjamin was beginning to think he was becoming an alcoholic, following in his father's footsteps.

As Doug drove them to the city, he reminded them that they would only have three days break before they would be heading back to the Island for another long stretch of work. He also told them that they would get their pay for the past ten days from the office, their destination, before he drove them to their respective apartments in the city. They would be paid in cash.

Benjamin needed to walk once he and Derek were dropped off at their home. He wasn't ready to go shopping with Derek. The truth was, he needed time to be alone. He needed a break from being with people even though he enjoyed and even liked his new work companions. Benjamin had learned that he could be a better part of a group if he somehow managed to take some quiet time along the way. It was as if the quiet time allowed him to breathe and make more space for being with others.

As he walked, a light drizzle was falling, but it wasn't about to deter Benjamin from walking towards English Bay. He carried a cheap umbrella that he had purchased on Vancouver Island. It was the Ben season in British Columbia and umbrellas were a must. Once he had reached the shore of English Bay, he picked up stones to throw into the water. The water was a bit too choppy for having the stones skip. A few minutes of watching stones disappear was all he managed before being distracted by the sounds of passing traffic in the rain. Benjamin's attention diverted, he decided that he would walk a bit further towards Stanley Park before heading back onto the busy streets of the downtown area. Too soon, the cold damp air had him reconsider his intentions. He retreated into the shelter of the streets in order to escape the cold wind coming off the water.

Strolling slowly down the streets and not having a destination in mind, he noticed various places he had seen with Céline last summer. He began to think that maybe it wasn't such a good idea to keep bringing the ghost of Céline into his life. He knew that Céline wasn't going to be in his life anymore. Shrugging, he walked on looking for a place to just sit and have a coffee. He had another hour to kill before he was to go to Ben and Jennie's for supper.

"Well, well," greeted Ben as Benjamin got off the elevator and walked towards the open door where his uncle stood with a welcoming smile. "You look like a drowned rat. Here, give me your umbrella and jacket."

"Hi, Uncle Ben," Benjamin said out of habit.

"Oh no, none of that uncle stuff, remember? Jennie will tear a strip off me if she hears you continue to call me uncle."

Grinning, Benjamin shook his uncle's hand and went into the apartment to say hello to Jennie who soon had him in a warm hug.

"What's this? Are you growing a beard?" she questioned with a bit of humor. "It looks good on you. Ben can't grow a beard or moustache if his life depended on it."

"Not really," answered Benjamin. "We worked late every day and it just seemed like such a waste of good sleeping time. I'll shave tomorrow after a good night's sleep."

"It looks good, Benjamin," she countered. "Why don't you leave it on for a while? See if you get used to it?"

"So," Ben interrupted, "How did it go? Are you going to stick with this job?"

"Ben?" reproved Jennie as she glared at her husband.

"Well," he responded defensively, "It's a good question."

"It's okay, Jennie. Yes, I like the job. And yes, I am sticking with it."

"Great!" replied Ben. "You can tell us all about it as we eat supper."

"Mmm, supper smells so good," complimented Benjamin.

With anticipation, Benjamin stood at the counter handing over two hundred dollars for a new guitar, an Aria six-string classical guitar. Having spent almost an hour playing it at the store, he knew he had to have it. It was the first time he had played a classical guitar and he fell in love with the mellow sounds that emerged as he picked and strummed. It wasn't a Gibson or Martin, but he knew he would never be able to spend that kind of money on a guitar. Besides, he reasoned to himself, he couldn't see himself doing without a guitar that long as it would take a lot more time to save that much money. Benjamin was looking forward to taking the guitar with him on the next road trip with his friends. Over the past several weeks they had become friends, not just work mates. With the payment made, Benjamin walked out of the store carrying the guitar in a new case and headed back to the house.

The break between road trips was shorter than usual this time. They had returned to Vancouver late yesterday afternoon and they were scheduled to be picked up tomorrow morning just after six. There wasn't much time to do anything other than washing clothes and put their latest earnings into the bank. After rent for February had been paid and now with the purchase of the guitar, Benjamin found that was still money left in his bank account. It was a good feeling. Benjamin had learned to live off his meal allowance which paid for groceries when back in Vancouver as well as restaurant and fast food meals on the road. Now that he had his guitar, there were no other planned expenses for the future to serve as a reason for saving his money; but, that was irrelevant. Benjamin knew he would continue living frugally and allow his savings to accumulate simply because he wanted to distance himself from poverty. Besides, he had learned from bitter experience that something always came along to mess up his plans. His savings were going to be his insurance.

Back in his room, he took out the new guitar and looked at it for several minutes, letting his fingers caress the surface before finally deciding to bring it to life. He sang softly as the songs began to unlock themselves from a place they had been hidden for the past two months. It felt like someone had opened up a cage in order to set him free. Benjamin played without thinking, played by instinct, by impulse as the words poured out to match the chords that had long ago been memorized by his fingers. He was unaware of the fact that others in the house had gathered at his open door, listening in silence. When he finally opened his eyes, he saw them and stopped in mid-song.

"Don't stop," pleaded a young man called Mike who lived in the room next to Benjamin's. "I'm sorry if I interrupted you. Do you want me to leave?"

"No, it's okay," Benjamin replied apologetically. "I was just surprised."

"Jeez," added a second voice, "I didn't know you could play guitar. I have a guitar but don't know how to play it. Maybe you could teach me sometime, eh?" A face emerged from behind Mike's back showing Benjamin who had just asked him about lessons. Brad lived on the upper floor and had heard the music while he was in the kitchen making himself a sandwich.

"Sure, Brad. No problem," offered Benjamin. "I can help you a bit when I'm at home. Why don't you get your guitar and we can start now," he encouraged.

"Thanks, man. I'm willing to pay for any lessons you give me," Brad promised. "Man, if only I could one day play like that."

While waiting for Brad to return, Benjamin sang another song, one that was more up tempo, one of his favorites, "Bobby McGee."

There was snow on the road as they turned onto Highway 28 in Campbell River. They had spent the previous night in Campbell River after inventorying two drugstores in the town. The crew were heading west to a town called Gold River which was about fifty-five miles away. It didn't seem far, but Doug told them that it would likely be at least a two hour drive in the snowy conditions and the twists and turns that didn't allow for speed even in good driving conditions. They were to inventory a gift shop and a grocery store in Gold River which meant they would be staying overnight there and returning to Campbell River late the next afternoon.

They followed along the Campbell River as they headed out of town and soon entered Elk Falls Provincial Park. The snow level deepened as they drove away from the coast, creating a magical scene in the heavy forest of the park. Then, the highway veered to the left leaving the river. The radio reception in the van became weaker prompting Doug to turn it off rather than have the crackle get on his nerves while navigating through the freshly fallen snow. A few vehicles had already passed this way leaving a trail that pointed the way. The road twisted and turned on itself as it skirted low mountains. A sign on the highway indicated the turn-off to McIvor Lake, but Doug kept the vehicle on the main highway. The crew hadn't been to Gold River before so each turn was a new discovery. However, it wasn't long before the scene became monotonous with the constant repetition of snow and trees with only a rare sign to indicate that they were actually heading in the right direction.

Jacqueline and Linda had brought their usual reading material, Betty was engrossed in some knitting project, and Derek was trying to sleep while Benjamin continued to maintain focus on the road. He had never been able to read or sleep in a moving vehicle though he had more than enough opportunities to do so over the years when his father had lead his family on countless road trips from Ontario to Alberta and back. Benjamin remembered one such trip which had taken them to Hay River through a snow storm. His memory was sparked by the almost hypnotic scene of snow and trees in constant movement.

Jacqueline set aside her novel and began to sing one of the current hits on the radio by Neil Diamond, Sweet Caroline. Soon everyone with the exception of Derek was singing along to her lead. One song followed another until Doug told them to look out the window at a small deer in the ditch. Derek appeared to stir from his self-imposed isolation to look before asking Benjamin to sing, Leavin' on a Jet Plane. Without thinking too much about why, Benjamin began to sing while the other's listened. Though he hadn't been on a jet plane before, the experience of leaving someone he loved brought a poignancy to the song that captured everyone's attention.

Living on the road as they had been doing for the past two months, evoked that same sense of regret at leaving others behind for all of them. When he finished singing no one said a word. All had sunk into their own private memories, all were wrapped in sadness. Benjamin, seeing the edges of depression on their faces, broke into another song, Maxwell's Silver Hammer by the Beatles. It wasn't long before all were laughing as they acted out the lyrics, "Bang, bang, Maxwell's silver hammer came down on her head." It came as a welcome surprise when Doug said they had reached Gold River. The sun was out and the streets were filled with deep slush as they pulled into the parking lot of the hotel which was to be home for the night.

Chapter Nine

It was April in Vancouver and Benjamin was on the last day of five days of break between road trips. Tomorrow they had to head back to work. It was a warm and sunny day as Benjamin found himself strolling through Stanley Park carrying his guitar. With the sun out, there already was a lot of other people taking advantage of the warm weather and the sunshine. Groups were picnicking, playing catch, and visiting as he passed them on the way to some place where he could lean against a tree, in the sunshine, and play his guitar. He passed a pond where a few ducks were already greedily eating bits of bread being thrown their way by two children who were supervised by their mothers or nannies. An old man who looked as if it still wasn't warm enough as he wore a heavy wool sweater with a warm cap on his head, sat at a bench reading a newspaper. Beside him, an older woman, likely his wife, was throwing seeds for squirrels to eat. It seemed as though the whole world was alive and well. Smiling, Benjamin decided to stroll along the walkway that edged the park until he was tired out. He wasn't in a rush.

In March he had begun to jog around the park as he felt out of shape from too many months of sitting in a van and long hours of work. He had decided that he was going to get into shape again. He loved running and realized that his avoidance of running the past few months had nothing to do with being busy at all. Though he enjoyed his work and the people he worked with, he had been living with an emptiness that they couldn't feel. But now, feeling better because of the return of music and running into his life, Benjamin was once again able to appreciate the simple pleasure of a warm and sunny day in the park.

Walking into the park, he saw a group of young people like

himself enjoying the moment. A gathering of young people were clustered around two young men who were playing guitars. On the edges of the group, a girl in a shiny, purple dress that made him think of silk, was dancing alone to their music. Benjamin watched her, intrigued at her lack of self-consciousness. Watching her, he approached and sat nearby as she continued to swirl and sway with the music. Benjamin joined in with the two guitarists knowing that it would be okay. All his experience at jam sessions had taught him that musicians loved to share the moment with others, feeding off each other through the music. They played, improvised and as time went on, more and more joined in to listen, or to dance with unconscious freedom.

When the unstructured concert ended, Benjamin noticed that the girl in the shiny, purple dress was still nearby. She was smiling which he took as an invitation for him to join her on the grass. She was the first girl he had talked to with the exception of his work mates, since he had lost Céline. She smiled at him with an enigmatic look that Benjamin mistook for interest in him as a young man. He didn't know that she was high on drugs. Benjamin's naivety was blinded by her pleasing shape, her long hair, and her smile.

Benjamin asked if she was hungry, if she wanted to go with him for a bite to eat. She told him she was starved so the headed off to buy a hot dog from one of the nearby street vendors. The conversation was one-sided with Benjamin doing most of the talking, something very unusual for him. Her contributions were her smiles, nods and occasional few words of agreement. Feeling brave, Benjamin invited her to go to his place, to his room. Once in the room, he had no difficulty in persuading her to make love to him. She didn't wear panties or a bra under her dress,. She was a flower child, a young woman that was as natural as one could be.

Benjamin made love to her again before he fell asleep in the afternoon sun that poured through his bedroom window. When he woke up, she was still in the bed, asleep. As Benjamin got up to go to the toilet, he noticed that the mess of love-making was still on her as it was on himself. He took a quick shower while wondering if he should wake her up so that she could also get cleaned up. Returning to his doorway, he saw that she was still sleeping so he decided to take care of hunger pangs. He went to the kitchen to make them both a late afternoon lunch as he hadn't eaten since breakfast that morning and he was sure that she would be as hungry as he was when she woke up.

When he began eating, the young woman emerged from the bedroom, naked and sticky and asked what there was to eat, asked if there was peanut butter and bread. Seeing her standing there without her purple dress, Benjamin noticed that she wasn't aware of her nakedness, either that or else she didn't care. Now that the spell of spring had broken, he knew that he had made a mistake in bringing her home. But not wanting to simply use her and send her off, he gave in to his guilt. He owed her. She wasn't some princess who was wise as well as beautiful as he had first thought out in the sunshine in the park. Rather, she was just another lost person. She had a woman's body, but not a woman's mind. He regretted instantly that he had given up his virginity to her.

She wouldn't have known or cared that he had been a virgin. It all seemed like such a waste. Yet, he had slept with her, entered her and left his semen in her and on her. For that, he knew he owed her, even if she wasn't yet aware of the fact.

Benjamin sent her to take a shower and told her he would make her some toast and peanut butter to eat while she cleaned herself up. He heard the water run in the bathroom and turned to making toast for her. When she returned several minutes later, wearing her dress which had lost its fairy tale allure, they ate in silence. Benjamin didn't know what to say and she didn't appear to have any need to talk. Her eyes were focused on the toast and peanut butter. It came as a surprise to Benjamin that he didn't know her name.

"Uh, I don't know if you remember, but my name is Benjamin, Benjamin for short," he began. "What's your name?"

Speaking with her mouth still busy chewing on toast she answered, "Jessica," before returning to the task of eating.

The silence was only broken by her munching and his occasional sips of coffee. Benjamin was hesitant to ask questions. Perhaps she was intending on leaving once she had eaten and didn't really want to talk about herself or what had happened between them.

"Uhm, Benjamin?" she asked as though unsure of his name.

"Yes?"

"Uhm, is it okay if I stay here with you?"

"Stay with me?"

"Yeah."

"Why do you want to stay with me? You don't even know who I am? I might not be a guy you want to stay with?" he asked puzzled by the request.

"It's, uh, it's like I don't have any place else to stay. You're nice and there's food. I don't have any money to get my own place. The last guy wasn't nice."

"Uh, well . . . "

"I won't eat too much. And," she added as though it was all that mattered, "you can have sex anytime you want. I don't have anywhere else to go."

Feeling guilty, Benjamin agreed that she could stay with him. When she was done her toast and peanut butter, she pulled him back into the bedroom, took off her dress before pulling down his pants and drawing him into her. Benjamin couldn't help it, he wanted and needed the sexual release, and all that he had denied himself when he was with Céline had come storming out in sexual need. Benjamin's body betrayed him as he responded to her open legs and the dark tangle where they joined.

While she slept again, Benjamin packed his bag for the next road trip. He had resigned himself to the young woman's presence though he knew that there was no love on either of their parts. As he packed his toiletries, he suddenly realized that he was officially now a man. He had just had intercourse with a woman. He wasn't a homosexual. Derek came in and saw Benjamin with a grin on his face and guessed what had just occurred.

"Is that grin about what I think it is?"

Benjamin nodded in response and then pointed to the bed through the opened door to his room. The girl was sprawled, naked on the top of the bed covers.

"You lucky little shit!" he exclaimed. "Where'n hell did you find her?"

Benjamin told Derek of seeing her in the park and of how she agreed to come back to the house with him and of their having intercourse. He didn't tell Derek about her being stoned on grass as he wanted Derek to think that she was interested in him as a man, not as a chick strung out on drugs willing to give it to anyone who would ask for it.

"Well, I'll be damned. You actually screwed a woman. Shit," he grinned, "Wait till I tell the girls that you're not a virgin anymore."

Derek didn't waste any time telling the girls the news.

"Derek," Betty said not even trying to disguise her distaste, "you're a pig." Looking at Benjamin with more than a little disappointment she added. "Men are pigs."

That seemed to be the end of the topic and the road trip continued to follow its normal flow with just one small change, a quietness of Jacqueline's part, a quietness and a distance in spite of outward behaviors which denied the distance.

When he returned from the road trip which saw him and Jacqueline take a side trip to Prince Rupert by plane to conduct two inventories there on their own, Benjamin was aware that something wasn't quite right with his body. There was a strange discharge coming from his penis and it burned. He began to suspect that whatever was wrong was because of the sex he'd had with Jessica. He knew that he would have to be tested for venereal disease. He planned on taking Jessica along with him so that they could both be tested and treated if necessary. He wasn't angry with Jessica as it wasn't as if she would have known. If they were going to continue living together and having sex, he wanted to make sure it was going to be safe.

He began to curse himself for not thinking of safety before. Why hadn't he used a condom? What if she was pregnant?

Moments after getting out of the van, Benjamin went to his room, Jessica wasn't there. Benjamin asked Mike who was at home, if she had just gone out, and when she was expected to return. Mike told him that she had left two days after Benjamin had left for the road trip. No one had heard from her or had seen her since then. Though feeling guilty for it, Benjamin breathed a sigh of relief. Now, all he had to worry about was getting himself tested.

Benjamin asked his aunt Jennie about where he could be tested for VD. She was a person he trusted with the question since she was a nurse as well as family. Jennie gave him directions to the nearest clinic and strict instructions to come to their place for supper that evening. They hadn't seen him for several weeks, a problem as far as she was concerned. Benjamin was the only family that both Ben and Jennie had in Vancouver.

The test results were conclusive, he had a mild case that was very treatable with antibiotics. Getting the prescription filled, Benjamin then headed back to the house where he sat discouraged and in discomfort. As the clock ticked away the hours, he stirred himself enough to wash up and change his clothes before heading over to Ben's and Jennie's for supper.

"Well, well," greeted Ben with even more than his usual enthusiasm. "Come in, come in. Supper is just on the table." Calling out to his wife he said, "Jennie, bring out the glasses and a bottle of wine, Merlot, I think. Benjamin is here."

Ben had never offered him wine before leaving Benjamin wondering what the celebration was all about. Maybe Ben had been given a promotion. It didn't take long to find out, for when the glasses were filled, Ben proposed a toast:

"Here's to Benjamin!"

Benjamin looked at his uncle with surprise. "Why are you toasting me?"

"Let me answer," Jennie said to Ben. He nodded and she continued. "When you were here with Céline, the two of you slept in the same bed. I knew that neither of you had extra clothes let alone pajamas. I also noticed that there were never any stains, no semen stains. So, for a long time both Ben and I thought that you were . . . "

"We thought you were gay," finished Ben. "Obviously, you're not gay. That's why the celebration. It might be a bit inappropriate, but we decided that it is something to celebrate. So, where is the lucky young woman?"

"I bet she fell in love with your mustache and goatee," added Jennie.

Feeling embarrassed, Benjamin told the truth of what had happened. He was sure that Ben would be angry, but he needed to be honest.

"Ah well," Ben said with a smile still evident on his face and in his mood. "A guy does have to sow a few wild oats."

At the end of May, Derek and Benjamin moved out of the house and into an apartment that was close to English Bay, less than two blocks from the beach. It was a one bedroom apartment. Derek wanted more independence than living in a communal house had to offer. The fact that there was a lot of turmoil in the house over the use of the house phone for long distance calls, a turmoil that didn't involve either Derek or Benjamin, but still made for a lot of tension in the house just added to the desire to leave. Derek agreed to pay the larger portion of the apartment's rent as he wanted the bedroom. Benjamin was to have the living room as his bedroom. It really wasn't a living room, rather it was a corner of the remainder of the apartment that opened out onto the balcony that faced the city rather than the water.

Benjamin knew that Derek wanted the bedroom in order to have more privacy as he had a steady flow of young women make their way to his bed whenever we were in the city. Benjamin's share was more than he had paid for the tiny bedroom in the house, but that was unimportant. His friendship with Derek was more important than saving a few dollars. Besides, he was still within walking distance of Ben and Jennie's who had become a lot closer to him that he would have ever predicted. Marriage had definitely changed Ben into a nicer person.

As he moved his stuff into the apartment, Benjamin noticed that he had acquired quite a few new clothes over the past five months in Vancouver. He was particularly proud of a beige buckskin jacket and matching suede leather cowboy boots. His collection of song booklets was growing as well. He had taken to playing more of Gordon Lightfoot's songs, as well as songs by Crosby, Stills, Nash and Young. His latest purchases were two books, one by Leonard Cohen and the other by Neil Young who had separated from his last group to go solo with a band called Crazy Horse. Benjamin's favorite songs were One Tin Soldier, Suzanne by Leonard Cohen, and Bridge Over Troubled Waters by Simon and Garfunkel. Benjamin had recently visited a couple of the coffee houses in the Gastown area of the city and had enquired about having the opportunity to perform at them. It looked promising. Only time would tell when and if he got that opportunity.

Since his first sexual experience, Benjamin had retreated from even trying to find a girlfriend in Vancouver. He had to admit that he was gun shy. The girls that Derek brought to the house were definitely not his type. Nor, as far as Benjamin could tell, were they Derek's type. With so many women making the pilgrimage to Derek's bed, Benjamin was beginning to think that all the younger women in BC were sluts, people you definitely didn't want to take home let alone spend a lifetime with. The only exceptions were the girls with whom he worked. And they deliberately made it a point to stay out of Derek's bed. Benjamin thought that perhaps if Jacqueline hadn't already had a boyfriend that perhaps she would be interested in him. However, for quite a while after Derek bragged about Benjamin losing his virginity, Jacqueline distanced herself from him. It had only been on the last road trip that she had begun to return to their old familiar relationship as very good friends. Still, Benjamin wondered if only he hadn't messed up, and if she didn't already have a boyfriend . . . "

With the weather becoming warmer, Derek and Benjamin began to spend a lot of their free time in the city on the beach. Derek was always in search of some unknown woman. Benjamin wondered what drove his friend knowing that it couldn't really be about the sex as Derek was never satisfied after they left his bed. He seemed to be driven in his search for something that was missing deep within himself.

About a week after they had moved in, Derek had met two girls on the beach, and as usual, he brought them to the apartment where he knew Benjamin was busy practicing for a gig in Gastown. He had persuaded the girls to come to the apartment to meet Benjamin, a famous folk singer from eastern Canada. Benjamin was working through his set, trying to narrow down his choices to five songs as Derek brought the girls into the apartment. When the girls heard the music, they became excited at meeting a professional folk musician, which is how Derek had described Benjamin. In a way it was somewhat the truth as Benjamin was getting paid to play and had played for money a fair number of times in the past. Still, it was stretching the truth.

When the door opened, they saw Benjamin holding his guitar as he turned the pages of a song book. It had been months since Benjamin had had a haircut and he had taken to wearing a goatee and moustache because Jennie liked them on him. For the girls, that was all the proof they needed and so they willingly entered the apartment. Benjamin was flattered at the attention and willingly put on a mini concert for them. When

Benjamin decided it was time for a tea break, Derek whispered into one of the girl's ears and soon both of them headed off to Derek's bedroom. It wasn't long before sounds of their sex play began to be heard.

The remaining girl looked at Benjamin awkwardly and took off her shorts and top revealing that she hadn't been wearing underwear. Benjamin was surprised but not really shocked by her actions. However, seeing her standing naked in front of him, shivering even though it was quite warm, Benjamin knew that she wasn't even sixteen years old. Her breasts were small and her pubic hair was just beginning to cover the cleft of her young womanhood. Benjamin couldn't find it in himself to take advantage of her even though she appeared to be expecting him to do so. She reminded him of his sister Béatrice at the age of fourteen, Shaking his head while still smiling, Benjamin told her she didn't have to have sex, that it would be fine with him if she put her clothes back on and had tea with him on the balcony. With evident relief, she put her shorts and tops back on and gratefully accepted a mug of tea.

Later, Benjamin began to wonder if he had been too stupid in passing up a chance for sex. He hadn't found any desire, or perhaps it was really, opportunity since his introduction to sex resulting in a case of the clap. But then his mind returned again to the vision of her vagina barely covered by pubic hair, the visible lips of her labia. Desire coursed through him, but not for the girl. Disgusted with himself for being turned on by a young girl not yet a woman, he turned back to the guitar for distraction and soon lost himself in the music.

Chapter Ten

Gastown was a seedy looking area in downtown Vancouver near the train tracks and Vancouver harbor. It was especially ugly in the daylight hours. Once the sun set however, the drunks and drug addicts disappeared into the shadows of doorways and back alleys. Neon lights then painted a different scene, one that promised gaiety, fine food and any entertainment that one could think of, legal or illegal.

Benjamin carried his guitar down Hastings Street and then turned onto Cambie Street where the coffee house he was to play in was located. Derek, Jacqueline, Betty and Linda walked along with Benjamin as they weren't going to miss his debut at the folk music club. Next to the coffee house was a restaurant from which they could hear jazz music. Benjamin was early. He was to play his set at nine-thirty, the second set of the evening, and it was only eight. As they entered the coffee house, he saw the duo that was to perform before him were already setting up for the opening set of the evening. Benjamin knew that he had to impress the audience as well as the owner. If the audience wasn't happy, then it would be unlikely that he would be asked back to play another set in the future.

"Not that many people here yet," Betty commented. "It seems busier next door."

Benjamin explained that the jazz music was supper entertainment and that a coffee house only became busy after people had finished dining. "I'm sure that this place will be packed so that there is no room left for latecomers," he added. "At least, it was the last time I was here."

"Place looks kinda neat," remarked Derek. "It sure is different from the Le Bistro club in Ottawa." Derek went on to describe Le Bistro to the girls while Benjamin put his guitar down at a table near the stage which was at the back of the coffee house. Benjamin then introduced himself to the duo, a young man and woman who had recently arrived from Winnipeg. The guy's name was Todd and he played a guitar and harmonica. His partner, Rita played a tambourine and did the vocals for the group. As they chatted, Benjamin asked about their set, which songs they were going to play so that he didn't end up doing any of the same songs. He was relieved when he found out that there wasn't going to be any duplication. Todd and Rita were doing songs by Joan Baez, Judy Collins, Joni Mitchell and one by Ben Dylan where Todd could showcase the harmonica. Benjamin let them know that he was focusing on Simon and Garfunkel, Gordon Lightfoot, Leonard Cohen and a different Dylan song. Wishing them luck, Benjamin returned to the table, ordered a coffee and enjoyed the company of his friends.

Benjamin's set came to an end much to his relief. He hadn't played poorly, but he knew that he hadn't played as good as he could have played. He just hadn't been able to add a fullness that comes with playing with emotion and passion. In his opinion, there hadn't been any technical mistakes, but there also hadn't been anything about his playing that would make people really want to listen. By the third song, he noticed that some of the people in the audience were focused on each other rather than on the stage. No one left or complained, but it didn't make Benjamin feel good to think that his playing had become nothing more than background music.

Jacqueline noticed Benjamin's unease and commented, "I enjoyed your songs, especially, It Ain't Me Babe. I didn't know you could play that song. You never played it on our trips."

"It used to be one that I used to play in Ottawa," Benjamin

replied, thankful that she hadn't mentioned the fact that the usual energy she heard at the hotels and motels that had been their home over the past few months, or when they were on the ferry, was missing. Derek knew. He saw the disappointment in Benjamin's face and suggested that they "blow the place."

As they left, Benjamin noticed a new singer setting up on the stage. Todd and Rita had left after their performance which hadn't gone well. Rita had been nervous and the vocals suffered. As she struggled, Todd had tried to fill in with more volume from his guitar, working the notes and riffs with greater intensity; and that had only made Rita more nervous. When they left the stage, Rita was crying and exited the coffee house at a run. The new singer was another woman, a couple of years older than Rita. It looked as though she had been here before as she nodded and smiled to various people in the audience who addressed her.

As he passed the counter, the owner called him over and gave him his share of the gate. It was more than he thought his performance was worth. And when the owner gave him a smile and said that he could come back for another set next week if he wanted, Benjamin's own smile became real. Perhaps he hadn't played as bad as it felt. Thanking the owner, he joined his friends on the sidewalk, waved the money that he had been paid and said with renewed enthusiasm, "Let's go party! I'm paying." With a whoop, the group walked off merrily down the street singing one of their road songs in loud voices causing passing pedestrians to turn and smile at them.

The dark blue and gray water of the Strait of Georgia was rolling in deep swells driven by a cold wind that had chased almost everyone into the shelter of the interior cabins of the ferry. Benjamin, Derek and Jacqueline stood along the rail looking downcast. Doug had just let them know that this was going to be the last trip for some time. Besides a few more inventories to do back in the Vancouver mainland area, there were no contracted audits on the books. When pressed, Doug told them that come the end of June, there were few places that wanted inventories taken. Whatever jobs did appear were easily handled by the Vancouver city crew which had been working for the company for the past three years. Doug suggested that they enjoy the summer and be ready to hit the road again after the September long week-end.

"There's no fricking way I can pay rent during the summer without a job," fumed Derek. "Were going to lose the apartment. Damn it all to hell!"

"Maybe we can find a different job for the summer?" suggested Benjamin with little enthusiasm.

Jacqueline interrupted to suggest, "You guys can always move into my place until you get another job and have enough money for your own place." Jacqueline lived in a basement suite of an older house in New Westminster, one of the suburbs of the city. In spite of their work friendship, the guys had never been to either of the girls' places. When they got together between jobs, they always met somewhere downtown.

"What will your boyfriend say?" Benjamin asked. "Don't you have to ask him first?"

"I live there alone," admitted Jacqueline. "I don't have a boyfriend."

"But you said. . . "

"I just didn't want you guys hitting on me all the time. It felt safer to simply tell the lie. I didn't know how to undo that lie once I got to know you guys. And, it didn't help when Derek celebrated you picking up a stoned girl and getting VD."

"Are you sure?" Derek asked.

"As long as you don't bring any chicks into the suite to screw. I don't want to come home and find you with some bimbo on my bed. Got it? Jacqueline said with heat, her words directed primarily at Derek.

"Yeah, sure," grinned Derek. "Loud and clear. No girls, no sex. When can we move in?

Benjamin looked at Jacqueline in a new light as she bantered with Derek, and wondered. But before going too far with his thoughts, he shook his head in an attempt to rid the as yet unformed thoughts from existence. Whatever might have been possible between them had been lost.

Agreeing to make the move, their mood improved. Jacqueline suggested a return to the inside of the ferry and joining Linda, Betty and Doug. Once inside with the group, no one mentioned the planned move of the guys into Jacqueline's. Even though they had paid their apartment rent until the end of the month, Benjamin and Derek agreed that they would move to Jacqueline's suite once they got back to the city. They had agreed to keep that information to themselves. Until then, they had another six days of work, with a return to Gold River for one of the jobs.

With the fact of this being their last road trip weighing heavily on the group, there was a change in their after work evenings. There was a reluctance to go to their rooms or wander off somewhere to do their own things. There was a need to stick together, and that included Doug. Evenings were spent at the bar, slowly sipping their drinks, usually the cheapest house draft. Doug repeatedly complimented them for being the best crew he had ever worked with over the years. Of the group, he was drinking the heaviest and would need help navigating the halls to his room for the night. The long drives from town to town were silent for the most part. No one had the will to sing as they nursed hangovers.

The last night was to be spent in Chemainus where there was a small job planned for the morning before they took the ferry back to the mainland. They arrived in Chemainus in the late afternoon and headed down to the pub just across the street from their motel, for a meal of fish and chips. The place was more of a dump than they were used to eating at; however, the place was busy and noisy. Country music was blaring from a juke box near the front entrance when they walked in. They saw an empty table with four chairs and claimed it. Derek rustled up two more chairs as they sat down and ordered house draft.

It wasn't long before the first glasses of beer were drained prompting Doug to order two pitchers of draft for the table. Not to be outdone, Derek added another two pitchers to the order. No one had yet ordered the fish and chips or had even thought of it. Benjamin was uncharacteristically drinking more than his usual two glasses of beer. By the time he was on his fourth glass, Jacqueline looked at him and shook her head before refilling her glass for her third. The noise level at their table increased as the beer disappeared. Benjamin signaled to the waiter to bring another two pitchers to their table before turning back and trying to sing along with the songs from the juke box even though he didn't know the words.

Doug began to tell them stories of trips taken in previous years with other crews, telling them of fiascos and wild times. He told them about one group who had spent most of their trips stoned on hash, so stoned that sometimes Doug had to invent inventory numbers based on previous years' totals. The stories brought out gales of laughter and the beer continued to flow. When Doug began to talk of his wife and two kids who had moved back to Abbotsford because of his long trips and his drinking, there were tears all around to match the tears on his face. At that point, Benjamin felt sick to his stomach, turned to the side and threw up on the floor. Ignoring the mess he made, he grabbed his glass of beer in an attempt to drink more. Everyone except Jacqueline laughed bringing an end to the maudlin mood that had built up when Doug had told his tale.

Jacqueline left her seat without a word, walked over to Benjamin and guided him out of his seat to the door and the fresh air. As soon as he stepped out the door, he threw up again. Wiping his mouth with the sleeve of her sweater, Jacqueline led him across the street to the motel and his room. Searching in his pockets, she found the key, opened the door and took him inside closing the door behind them. She took him straight to the washroom, gave him a glass of water, and knelt beside him while he upchucked whatever was left inside of him. After a while, he settled back onto his heels, slumped against her while holding onto the toilet.

Jacqueline got up, and helped Benjamin to his feet and then began to undress him, throwing his soiled clothes into the corner. Taking a cloth, she wiped his face and led him to one of the beds where she pulled down the covers and had him lay down. No sooner had his head settled on the pillow, then he fell asleep. She looked at him for a few moments and then lay beside him in her clothing. After a few minutes, she needed to go to the bathroom. Once done, she decided she needed a shower to get rid of some of the vomit that had sprayed onto her. After showering, she wrapped the towel around herself and slipped back into the bed and held onto Benjamin who lay with his back to her. And, she slept.

She woke as light began to filter in through the window. Benjamin was still sleeping as she put on her clothing. Derek lay on the other bed still in his clothing, snoring. Opening the door as quietly as possible, she crossed the hallway to go into her own room. She had a room to herself as Linda and Jennie shared a room. The girls had been taking turns having a room to themselves as they went from one motel to the next. Once inside, she went to the bathroom and ran the tub while she took a pee. Laying in the tub, letting the warm water soothe her, she began to cry softly.

The group stopped at one of the grocery stores in the town before heading to the ferry. The hangovers had disappeared for the most part. While they bought fruit, sandwich meat and buns, Doug had gone off on his own saying he would be back to pick them up in twenty minutes. Benjamin grabbed a package of raisin bran muffins and packages of sliced smoked meat and ham for sandwiches. Derek bought a half dozen large buns, and a few bags of chocolate chip cookies. Betty bought a huge watermelon, Linda bought a selection of juices and pop, and Jacqueline bought a basket of cherries and a basket of strawberries. On the ride back to Vancouver they were going to be a picnic, celebrating the months together and their friendship.

As Doug pulled up, they all piled into the van with their purchases. It was an hour and a half to the ferry terminal at Sidney and because everyone was hungry, Benjamin passed out the muffins and Jacqueline doled out strawberries so that the edge would be taken off their appetites until they were on the ferry. Strangely, in spite of the fact that they were still feeling a bit down, Doug was whistling and smiling. Something was up.

The trip went quickly enough and the van soon made its way onto the ferry which was moving more than usual. The wind had picked up and the swell was lifting and lowering the ferry during the boarding process. When Doug had parked the van and turned off the engine, he turned to the group and announced that he had booked them a room on the ferry, a private room, for their picnic. The announcement brought a round of applause and smiles. They wouldn't have to worry about noisy kids and nosy people during their meal. They then made their way up the narrow stairs onto the upper of the two levels for passengers where Doug had booked their private room. It was a glassed-in room which allowed them to look out onto the sea, as well as the passenger lounge.

As Linda and Benjamin made the buns into sandwiches, Betty and Jacqueline cut up the watermelon. Derek's help was reduced to opening the bag of cookies and eating them while waiting. While they were occupied with these tasks, Doug had left to take care of a bit of business. The ferry was being tossed around on the waves making it a bit difficult to stand without holding onto a support.

Doug returned followed by another man wearing a uniform that said he was a ferry employee, who carried a large, brown paper bag. Doug thanked the man who gave him the bag as he left, Doug then opened the bag taking out a package of plastic cups, a carton of orange juice, large bottle of tonic water and two bottles of gin and a large pitcher. Derek immediately offered to help and between them had mixed drinks for everyone, mixing a third of a glass full for each of them. A large pitcher of mixed drink was made ready for later. It was hard to pour more than that into a glass at a time because the ferry was pitching in the rough waters as they entered the open part of the channel crossing.

Doug called everyone to take a glass of the gin, tonic and juice and told them of a ritual he had learned from one of his friends in Vancouver, a Chinese lad who had worked on one of his crews a few years earlier. He wanted the group to do the toast Chinese style which he called "gan bei." He then explained that basically it was "bottoms up" with a little twist at the end where they had to hold their cups upside down and bow to the others to whom the toast had been offered. That gesture was to honor those being toasted. Doug went on to explain that typically, Chinese would then take turns making toasts so that in the end, everyone had an opportunity to honor everyone in the group.

Grinning, the group were ready for the toasts that followed. Doug began: "I hope you don't mind, but I have adopted all of you as my children," which brought out a flurry of protests that they were too old to be his children. "No, no, you guys aren't too old at all. My son is twenty-four and my daughter is twenty two. Like I said, I think of you as family. So, my toast is to all of you guys. To you, my family! Now, gan bei!" Draining his cup, he then held his cup upside down and bowed to them. The group looked at each other then lifted their cups and repeated his shout of gan bei.

Toast followed toast in quick succession, each time with the cups refilled for the next toast. Since the gin had been mixed, no one got too drunk in the process. With toasts done, the group dove into the watermelon. Without thinking about it, the glasses were again refilled with periodic new toasts surfacing. Outside the waves became bigger and there was even more difficulty in standing without stumbling from one side to the other which was made even worse as the effects of the gin began to be pronounced.

Benjamin began to think that he would throw up like he had the night before and ruin it for everyone, so he cut back to only putting a very small amount in his plastic cup for each succeeding toast. He made sure to eat as much watermelon as he could to dilute the alcohol even more, knowing that if he tried to eat a sandwich that he would vomit it all and ruin the party. No one was eating the sandwiches. Derek had eaten most of the cookies, sharing some of them with whomever wanted one. Jacqueline looked green and complained of sea-sickness which was a surprise as she was the only one besides Derek and Benjamin who escaped being sea sick on rough crossings between the Island and the mainland which occurred too frequently as far as Linda and Betty were concerned.

As they approached the ferry dock at Tsawwassen, the group carefully made their way down the stairwell to the car deck. Derek supported Jacqueline afraid that she would fall, while Benjamin held onto the stair railing and slowly descended. Somehow, only Doug seemed to be not feeling the effects of the gin. He told the group that he would pick them up again the next day in order to take them to the office for their last pay. He didn't want the bosses to see them so obviously under the influence of alcohol. He decided that it would be best to drop off Jacqueline and the boys first before she got sick in the van. No one argued.

Closing the door behind them, Derek headed to the little kitchen in search of food. Jacqueline rushed to the bathroom and the sounds of her retching echoed into the living room area which also served as a bedroom for Derek and Benjamin. Benjamin, hearing Jacqueline vomit rushed out the door into the yard and was soon depositing his vomit into the flower bed.

Waking up with a splitting headache, Benjamin vowed he would never get drunk again. Derek had gone and left a note saying he would be back by two, the time that Doug was supposed to return and take them to the office for their final pay cheque. Jacqueline was still sleeping so he kept as quiet as he could as he opened the small fridge in search of something to drink, hopefully there would be some ginger ale or coke if not juice. Filling a glass with milk, the only choice available, he turned to walk back to the table and saw Jacqueline just getting out of bed. She was nude. He had seen her nude quite often in saunas over the six months they had worked together, but seeing her nude in her bedroom felt like he was invading her privacy. Quickly he turned his head and walked to a different part of the room so that she could have her privacy. Still nude, Jacqueline walked into the bathroom, ran the tub, and took a long pee before crawling into the tub. She hadn't closed the bathroom door, probably used to having complete privacy in her basement suite.

As she was starting to get out of the tub, she asked Benjamin if he wanted to use the water before she drained the tub. If so, he'd better hurry into the tub before the water got too cold. She was toweling off as she addressed him. Benjamin said sure, took off his clothes and entered the tub while Jacqueline ignored him, a fact that Benjamin appreciated as his penis began to wake up. Jaqueline continued to dry off and then brush her hair and teeth before putting on a light layer of makeup. Benjamin looked at her while trying not to be too obvious. It was only when Jacqueline looked at his swollen penis that he got self-conscious, feeling guilty for his thoughts. Jacqueline smiled at his embarrassment, bent and gave him a kiss on the cheek and then left the bathroom. A few minutes later she called out and asked him if he wanted some eggs or cereal.

The next few days were some of the happiest days Benjamin could remember having in a long time. Earlier in the evening, he had again performed at the coffee house, this time at a later time slot, playing three extra songs. His song choices were more upbeat to match his positive frame of mind. Only Jacqueline and Derek went to the coffee house with him now that they were done with inventories for the summer. Both Linda and Betty had left the city the afternoon they had picked up their last pay. They didn't say where they were going or when, or even if, they were going to return. Benjamin knew that it might have been the last time he would ever see them.

He didn't think they would be back for the fall to work with them.

When Benjamin returned to the table where Derek and Jacqueline sat, she squeezed his hand and smile as she told him how good he sounded. She had been listening to him practice twice a day in preparation for the gig. She had helped him choose from the songs he practiced the songs he had just sung to the audience.

Derek noticed her giving Benjamin's hand a squeeze before she released it to reach for her drink. He saw that something was building between them even if they weren't yet aware of it. He felt like the proverbial third wheel and knew that he would have to leave. It was hard and painful to think about for him. When Benjamin had left the previous summer, Derek had slipped into a depression that only was banished when Benjamin had reappeared in September. Derek had been a lone wolf too many years after his best friend had moved with his family out of Hull, Quebec at the end of grade five.

This time, it was going to have to be him who would leave. There was no way he could stay and watch whatever it was that was coming to life between Benjamin and Jacqueline. When Benjamin had been with Céline it had been different. He knew from the beginning that Benjamin hadn't fallen in love with her. No matter how long they had gone out, it had been to him that Benjamin always turned as he suffered so often through that doomed relationship. Benjamin had emptied out his soul to him time and time again. And now, it was all going to come to an end. He needed to leave before that happened.

With these thoughts racing through his mind, Derek interrupted their chatter about the performance. "I'll be leaving on Monday," he announced.

"Leaving to go where?" asked Benjamin with interest not realizing that when Derek said leaving that it meant not coming back.

"I'm going to go home to Ottawa and see how my mother is doing."

"You know how she's doing," Benjamin replied with some confusion. "You just talked to her three days ago on the phone."

"Yeah, I know," he admitted, "but it's something I just need to do. If I wait too long then we'll get too busy here again and then another whole year will have passed. She doesn't need to have me totally abandon her like my Dad."

Derek's statement brought a pall over the table.

"I have to go with him," Benjamin told Jacqueline. "Can't you see he's depressed? I'm worried that he do something stupid and never make it home. Besides, I should go and see my brothers and sisters and let them know I'm still alive." Since he had left Ottawa, Benjamin had never even phoned his home. He had sent letters and an occasional cheque to his mother in hopes that somehow it would be spent on the kids.

"Benjamin, why do you have to go?" pleaded Jacqueline

"Can't you see?" Benjamin asked with frustration. "It's the only way I can make sure he is okay, and that he comes back to Vancouver.

"God are you blind. He doesn't want to share you," she complained with bitterness.

"That's absurd!" retorted Benjamin. "He's just hurting. You just don't know Derek."

Over the past few days, Benjamin had disclosed his past to Jacqueline, about his dysfunctional family, about Céline, and about the poverty that he had lived in as he grew up. She accepted everything he told her without seeming to be too surprised, without retreating back as if he was somehow a liability. She told him about her past as well, about her ex-boyfriend who beat her, about her step-dad who raped her, and about her mother who was an alcoholic. Like him, she was damaged goods.

"We'll come back after we've seen our families. We'll only be gone a couple of weeks. I do have another gig to play in three weeks, I just have to do this Jacqueline."

Somehow, though unstated by Jacqueline, she saw that they had entered into a relationship that had crossed from friendship to something more but as yet undefined. Benjamin hadn't yet clued into the change. His mind wasn't ready for a relationship yet and so he couldn't see and respond to Jacqueline's need. Jacqueline was beyond frustration as he just wasn't understanding her signals. She wanted him to crawl into her bed every night, had wanted that almost from the first time they had met just before Christmas. She just couldn't believe that he had never picked up on it. He either had to be the most naïve guy she had ever met, or he simply didn't want a relationship with her. God it was so frustrating. And truthfully, Jacqueline had to admit that his naivety, his air of unconscious innocence was what drew him to her.

Jacqueline was worried that once he walked out the door, he would never come back. Perhaps she had told him too much about her history and that was why he was leaving, she tried to convince herself otherwise, but it wasn't working. Though she didn't feel worthy of him. Biting back her negative thoughts, she knew that she was being unfair in thinking that Benjamin was leaving because of what she had told him of her history.

Her past didn't influence anything about the way Benjamin held her in high regard. The best she could do, now, was to hope that he did come back and that he eventually would catch on that she loved him.

"I'll be here," she stated with no enthusiasm and little hope. "When you get back, you can stay with me again."

With a grin, Benjamin promised, "Great! I'll be back in time to celebrate my twenty-first birthday. Be ready to party, girl!"

And so it was, on the last Monday of June, Benjamin and Derek pulled on their backpacks, with both giving Jacqueline a kiss on her cheeks and with spoken good-byes, and then left.

Part Three

Summer on the Road

Chapter Eleven

They caught a ride south to White Rock and only had to wait less than fifteen minutes to get a second ride to the border crossing at Blaine, Washington. Both of the boys carried a pup tent, sleeping bag, and clothes with Benjamin also carrying his guitar. Knowing that there would likely be cool days, Benjamin had taken his buckskin jacket and suede boots which he was wearing as they waited to be cleared by American border security as it was quite chilly in spite of the sunshine. Benjamin was the first to be asked questions and was soon cleared to cross the border. However, Derek was having problems and was losing his cool. In typical Derek fashion, he had said something sarcastic to the officer, and as a result, his backpack was emptied onto the pavement and every item looked at carefully before being discarded haphazardly onto the pavement. Benjamin was surprised that they had checked Derek out as he was the clean cut one of the two. Benjamin had more of a hippy look with his longish hair and beard. Once Derek had gathered his stuff together and repacked it, he turned and waved and gave the border guard a big smile.

"Now why did you want to cut through the States to get home again?" asked Benjamin with a laugh.

"Shut up, smart ass!" he grinned in response. "Let's see if some beautiful chicks will stop and give us a ride," he continued as he stood at the edge of the highway with his thumb stuck out.

Their next ride was yet another older guy who was only going as far as Bellingham where they decided was a good spot to have lunch. As usual, they settled on a cheap burger and fries at Macdonald's. The weather had improved so Benjamin strapped his jacket onto the top of his sleeping bag as they sat at a table outside of the small restaurant. Once the straps were secured, Benjamin sat back and ate his cheese burger.

Derek had already begun to chat with two girls who were sitting at the next table. In almost a matter of moments, he turned to Benjamin and said, "Let's go sit at their table. They've got a car and are going on a camping trip through the mountains. They said we could join them if we wanted to."

"I thought we were going to Seattle tonight?" responded Benjamin.

"Seattle's just a place. We go with them, we'll get to Spokane the scenic way."

They drove for five hours before deciding to set up camp at Sun Lakes' campground. While the guys set up their two pup tents, the girls set up a larger tent which they shared. Then, a campfire was started and hot dogs were roasted. Before leaving Bellingham, the girls had bought enough food to last for at least three days. Once the meal was finished, Benjamin pulled out his guitar and played with both girls singing along with him while they cleaned up the few dishes that had been used. Derek was poking the fire with a long stick, turning over the logs every few minutes to see if he could get the blaze to go higher. With darkness arriving, Benjamin put away his guitar and joined the others around the fire, and sipped on a coke. In the silence, they listened to the crackling of the fire, the occasional popping and hissing adding to the symphony of a campfire.

Benjamin noticed that Derek was holding the hand of one of the girls as they slipped away from the fire and headed into the tent. The other girl looked at him and smiled while she said, "I guess I'll be staying out here for a while."

"I could use the company, Patti," offered Benjamin. "It sure is beautiful out here. Look at all the stars."

"You play well," she complimented.

"Thanks."

"Are you cold?" she asked as she moved closer to him

"No. I don't get cold too easily," he said with his eyes peering into the flames that were now blue and small, a contrast to the blackened and cracked patchwork of the logs that were much smaller.

As he poked into the cracks, Patti snuggled next to him and gave a little shiver. "Brr! It's getting cold out here. Time to go into the tent and crawl into a sleeping bag."

He replied. "I think I'll stay out here for a bit longer and make sure the fire is out." Turning and giving her a smile, he said, "Night, Patti."

The next day, they set off after a breakfast of sausage and eggs and coffee. With only a brief stop in Spokane, they drove on stopping for a picnic at a small place called Sandpoint where they enjoyed walking barefoot along the edges of the lake. Then, they continued their journey with another stop at Kalispell for a few more groceries just before their campground destination called Sundance.

Patti and her friend Jill decided to make hash browns to go with the small steaks purchased in Kalispell. Derek, as usual, occupied himself with the fire while Benjamin roasted four corn cobs in the ashes at the edge of the fire. When supper was done, Derek helped Jill with the dishes while Patti sat beside Benjamin, singing along with the old folksongs and some of the pop songs that were popular on the radio.

After a while, while everyone was still sitting around the fire, Benjamin got up, said good night and then went into his little tent. He didn't want to relive another uncomfortable situation like the night before when Patti had been so obvious about wanting him to sleep with her. As he lay in the darkness, still hearing the crackle of the fire, he began to wonder just what it was that he was doing in the States, camping with two strangers. There didn't seem to be any sense in just wandering. If they were supposed to be going home to Ottawa, what were they doing just travelling half days up and down mountain highways stopping simply to stop and be tourists? He heard Jill and Derek head into the larger tent and the sounds of sex soon following. When things quietened down, he heard Patti go into the tent.

"Thanks, girls. It was fun," said Derek as he and Benjamin got out of the car in Browning, Montana. "We're heading north from here," he explained to them as their reason for leaving them. The girls had wanted them to travel on with them to Great Falls, Montana and then on to Yellowstone National Park. However, Derek had already tired of Jill, especially of her clinginess. Benjamin was relieved to be leaving the girls as well. Maybe now they could now focus on the journey back to Ottawa.

Browning was a very small town, one filled with false-front stores and a hotel along a dusty road. They found a café and bought some coffee. The place reminded Benjamin of television programs about the Wild West such as Bonanza and Gunsmoke. The few patrons in the café were dressed in jeans, long-sleeved cowboy shirts and were wearing cowboy boots. Two men, wearing cowboy hats, looked at the boys making them feel uncomfortable. Benjamin suggested that they leave even though they hadn't finished their coffee. Walking out of the café, they were made more nervous as the two cowboys followed them out, sat on a bench and watched them as they put on their backpacks and hustled down the street.

After more than an hour of passing half tons and cars passing them, a trucker finally stopped to give them a ride. "You guys are lucky that you got a ride before dark. They don't like hippies in small town Montana."

The ride was just over an hour from Browning to Shelby where the trucker was headed. As the miles raced by, Benjamin noticed white crosses in the ditches from time to time and asked about them.

"Accidents. Each cross indicates that someone had died there in a car accident."

Arriving in Shelby, they asked the driver where the town's campsite was located. They didn't want to pitch their tents out in the country somewhere as the images of "Easy Rider" kept coming into their minds. Derek and Benjamin had seen the movie at a cinema in Vancouver earlier in the year. The passing countryside and the passing half-ton trucks with rifles displayed in rear-window racks was just too unnerving.

They began to head down the street towards the campgrounds which were several blocks away when a police car stopped beside them.

"Hey, you!" called out the cop, "Where do you think you're going?" he grilled them as though they were suspects for some recent crime.

"We're just going to the campground," explained Benjamin before Derek could say something stupid and really piss off the cop.

"No, you're not. Get in the car, I'm taking you two down to the station."

"Why?" Benjamin asked somewhat confused. "What did we do wrong? Why can't we go to the campground? We're just Canadian tourists."

"Get in, now!" commanded the policeman as he got out of the car with his gun pulled out to reinforce the command. "We'll find out at the station who you really are."

The boys were taken to the sheriff's office where they ended up sitting on a hard bench for two hours while waiting for the interrogation they knew was coming. While they waited, the police had contacted border patrol in order to see if they were on the list of drug dealers to watch out for, or if they had escaped from some work prison in Canada. Finding nothing they could use, the cop who had brought them in, took them into his office.

"You two can go to a café for a bite to eat while we are waiting for another report. Don't you dare bugger off until I say you can."

He then let the boys go with the warning not to leave town, but to come back in a couple of hours to find out what was to be done with them. Shaking, the boys walked out of the police station with their bags to a pub two blocks down the street where they sat at a table and ordered a pitcher of draft.

"God, this stuff tastes like piss," complained Derek.

"I don't like this," Benjamin whined. "Let's leave. There's a bus station just across the street. Maybe there's a bus leaving soon that will take us into Canada?"

"Good idea," replied Derek pushing the beer aside. "Come on. Let's go check it out."

They only had to wait another twenty minutes before a bus

was leaving for Lethbridge, Alberta, a two and a half hour trip including clearing customs at Coutts. They bought tickets for Milk River which was just over an hour away as they didn't want to spend too much money on bus tickets. As soon as they took their seats on the bus, they let out a cautious sigh of relief as they saw the cop car driving slowly down the street as if looking for them. That relief turned in whoops of joy as they cleared the Canadian border check without difficulty. They had even been told, "Welcome back home," from the border guard who checked their ID.

Getting off the bus in Milk River, they immediately went back to the highway intent on hitching a ride into Lethbridge. When a car did stop and they found out the driver was headed to Calgary, they decided that they would go all the way with him. He was on his way to the Stampede and when he saw Benjamin's suede jacket and cowboy boots, he assumed that that was where they were going as well.

"So, are you playing at one of the bars for the week?" asked the driver whose name was Ed.

"I'm hoping to," lied Benjamin. "Any suggestions?"

"I dunno," reflected the driver. "There are a few places on 17th Street you might wanna try. Say, where are you guys staying?"

"No plans yet, admitted Derek. "Perhaps at a hostel. Do you know of any hostels in Calgary?"

"Well, there's one just on the corner of 17th and MacLeod Trail, just across the street from the Stampede grounds. I can let you guys off there. I going into the north end of the city to stay with my sister in Hillhurst."

"Cool," Benjamin said, "Thanks a lot. We sure do appreciate

all the help you're giving us."

"Well, how about a song or two on that gee-tar. It'd sure help the miles pass a lot quicker."

Benjamin played some old country and western songs he had learned four years earlier when he played in his uncle's band in the Ottawa and Hull region. He even remembered a few older songs that seemed to please their driver, songs such as Tom Dooley, Wolverton Mountain, and King of the Road.

It was still light out when Ed let them off across the street from the hostel. They were lucky to each get a bunk in the crowded room because of the Stampede. Derek suggested that they stay two nights so that they could check out the last day of the Stampede. Benjamin would have rather continued their journey, but decided since they had travelled more than had been hoped for finally agreed.

They had heard that the fair was moving on to Edmonton from some people at the Calgary fair grounds, and giving in again to pressure from Derek, they headed north getting as far as Red Deer. Their ride was heading on to Sylvain Lake and suggested they might enjoy the lake, also suggesting that Benjamin could make a few dollars playing at the beach bar. Knowing that there was time yet to get to Edmonton for the Klondike Days, Benjamin and Derek went with their driver to Sylvain Lake.

It was just after noon when they arrived at the beach confectionary and restaurant where their driver let them off. The boys decided to have an early lunch before setting up their tents in the nearby campgrounds. While at the counter, ordering lunch, Benjamin asked about playing at the beach bar, wondering if there were any openings. He was given a name and told that the bar owner would be at the bar at three that afternoon, and that he could best answer Benjamin's questions. It wasn't as if he needed the money, but it wouldn't hurt to earn a bit extra knowing that he wouldn't be getting another paycheck until sometime in September.

Once the tent was set up, Benjamin headed towards the bar while Derek wandered around the cottage grounds. They agreed to meet again later in the afternoon and cook their own supper, another effort at saving some of their limited resources. Benjamin sat outside the bar on one of the benches by the beach waiting until the owner showed up, watching kids play in the dark sand, going up and down the tall slide into the water and chasing each other around as they splashed as much as possible. It looked like they were having a lot of fun. Finally, the owner appeared and Benjamin asked about playing a music set for him.

"Well, let's see. How does Thursday sound to you? You can play as many songs as you want as no one else is playing that night."

"It sounds great, sir," Benjamin said appreciatively. "How much do you pay?'

"Well, I don't pay anything, of course," he answered. "You get what the customers give you in tips for playing. You make 'em happy and you make good money. You make 'em happy and I make good money as well. Sorta sounds fair to me. What do you think?"

"Yeah, sounds fair. I'll be here. What time do you want me there?"

"Nine o'clock is early enough. Maybe ten is even better. More people here after it gets dark."

Pleased with himself for arranging a performance for two nights later, Benjamin returned to the tent site and changed into a pair of shorts. It was hot, very hot. He didn't have a bathing suit, as he hadn't needed one the whole time he worked with the crew. No one except the crew ever used the pools and the saunas at the cheap motels that they stayed in on the Island. The shorts would have to do for now. Walking along the edge of the lake with the water halfway up to his knees, the desire to swim disappeared. Too many kids and too much noise taught him that it would be better to swim in the evening when the kids were back in their cottages or at the campgrounds. He walked back to the tent in time to meet Derek who was already there.

Benjamin told him of the deal with the owner of the bar which pleased Derek as he wanted to relax for a while, take a break from hitch-hiking. The boys then began to talk about skipping out Edmonton for a few extra days at the lake before heading east. The took out a map and planned their route for when they left before building a small fire and cooking smoked sausages for their supper.

As usual, Benjamin spent the evening playing his guitar. And, as usual, he soon had a small audience, mostly curious kids who wandered over to see the hippy playing. As darkness began to close in, a woman in her thirties came to get two of the kids, two boys, telling them that it was bed time. They protested as kids always protest at bedtime. And typically, she told them, "Okay, one more song and then you have to go to the cottage." She sat down on a nearby bench and listened while she waited for the kids.

"Please, Mom, one more, one more?" pleaded the boys.

"Okay, one more," she agreed.

One more song turned into three more songs. Derek sat beside her and made small talk between the songs while Benjamin asked the kids which song they wanted him to play next. Finally, the mother took her boys to the cabin saying good night and thanks to Derek and Benjamin.

The next day, Derek moved in to the cottage at the invitation of the boy's mother. Their father, a farmer, was busy in the fields, haying. The family was at the lake for four weeks without him and she was hungry for attention which Derek was only too willing to give her. It seemed strange that a woman more than ten years older would want to get involved with Derek, but it happened. While the boys were playing at the beach all afternoon, they were in her bedroom with the screen door locked so that the boys didn't return and catch them. Again, when the boys were sleeping, the two lovers would spend time in bed. On

Thursday evening, Derek didn't go to the bar with Benjamin. It was as if he had been caught in a spider's web with the spider feeding off his youth.

Benjamin set up on a small stage near the entrance of the bar so that the music would draw any passers-by. He began with a tune of Gordon Lightfoot's before switching to one by Neil Young which he followed up with a Simon and Garfunkel song. Few people seemed to be paying attention as the talk continued at the bar and tables. He shifted to a Beatles song only to have someone shout out, "Can't you play any real music?" Others took up his call and asked for country music. Seeing that his plans for the concert were crashing all around him, Benjamin quickly did a shift to the country songs he remembered. Only then, did the mood in the bar improve. Sometimes he struggled with tunes barely remembered but that didn't seem to bother the audience who were still loud, but now satisfied.

Benjamin decided to try a second set and asked if any of the ladies in the audience wanted to join him on the stage and sing. A guy from the back of the bar shouted out "Sheila!" and others began to chant her name. Benjamin asked her which songs she wanted to sing and if she knew the key for the song. Thankfully she knew the key allowing Benjamin to follow her vocal lead. Country music was notorious for using few chords in their songs. Once you knew the key, it was easy to know the progression of chords. Between verses, he was able to pick out a few complimentary notes which met with approval all around.

At the end of the set, the owner sent a hat around the room. When it came back to him, he counted out the money and pocketed half of it. Still, it was enough money to pay for the camping fees, perhaps a new set of strings and with a little left over. Pocketing the money he packed up his guitar and was on his way out the door when he saw Derek wave him over to his table, just inside the door.

"I didn't know you were here?" commented Benjamin, glad that Derek had seen at least some of the performance. "When did you get here?"

"Near the end of your first set when you were singing a Johnny Cash song."

"You're not with Elaine?"

"Nope. One of her kids woke up and wandered into the bedroom and saw us going at it. Elaine lost it, yelled at the kid to go back to bed and then threw me out. She's got problems now, as if she didn't already have problems. Man, she's insatiable. She was wearing me out," he laughed.

"I guess that means we head out tomorrow, doesn't it?"

grinned Benjamin.

"Yep, that it does, mate. That it does.

Chapter Twelve

The next day they only made it just over two hundred and fifty miles by late afternoon to a town called Kindersley in Saskatchewan. They found the campgrounds on the east side of the town. Not wanting to risk getting stuck in the middle of nowhere, they decided to pitch their tents in the campgrounds which were barely more than a rough pasture filled with gopher holes, two outhouses, and a scattering of picnic tables. There wasn't a single tree on the grounds. The six picnic tables with fire pits were the only evidence that it was indeed a campground. Putting their backpacks inside their tents, they walked back into town, with Benjamin taking along his guitar. They went in search of something to eat and found a dingy Chinese restaurant that had cheap food. Derek put a quarter into the juke box and selected three songs from the list which was only country music.

When they had finished eating their rice, chop suey, and greasy egg rolls, they sat back drinking their warm pop and wondered about how the owner stayed in business. The food was bad and they were the only customers in the restaurant. Finished with their pop, they wandered down the few streets of the town in search of the pub because Derek wanted a beer before they head back to their tents for the night. Unlike the Chinese restaurant, the pub was crowded and noisy, too crowded for Benjamin's liking. As they squeezed in to stand by the long counter, Benjamin placed his guitar between his knees and the counter so that it wouldn't get kicked by accident. Eventually the bar keep served them. He didn't even ask for ID when they placed their order for two cold glasses of beer.

It was ten thirty when they arrived back at the campsite.

"Shit!" Derek exclaimed. "What 'n hell happened?" Their tents had been turned upside down with the tent pegs scattered along with the contents of their back packs. While they had been in town, some local youth had trashed their site.

"Jeez," groaned Benjamin. "I bet it was those three guys near the door making comments about us being hippies."

They picked up their things, and decided to walk a few miles before setting up again along one of the less travelled side roads next to a pasture.

From Kindersley, they made good time the next morning to reach Saskatoon. It was Benjamin's twenty-first birthday, he was now able to legally buy beer though it hadn't been a problem the whole time he had been in BC and while they were hitch-hiking. Because it was still early in the day, they decided to take a city bus to the highway going south to reach the Trans Canada. Another ride soon came along and took them to Regina. Derek wanted to continue on hoping to catch a ride to Winnipeg as he was still upset with having their campsite trashed the night before. It was close to supper hour when a car stopped and offered them a ride to Balgonie, a small town about twenty miles east of Regina.

At the edge of the town, they stood for almost two hours hoping for a ride. It was getting dark and they knew that they weren't going to be catching a ride at this time of the day, so they walked into the town hoping to find a campground for the night. No campground was to be found. Derek then suggested that they go to the Catholic Church and ask there for a bed for the night. Benjamin, was very hesitant to go along with the idea though he couldn't say why he wasn't in favor of the idea. Derek pushed until Benjamin agreed.

They walked up the sidewalk to the priest's house which was

149

beside the church, and Derek knocked on the door. He explained that they were Catholics who needed a place to stay for the night. He added that they were hitch-hiking home to Eastern Canada. As the priest hesitated, Derek also told the priest that it was Benjamin's twenty-first birthday. That seemed to make all the difference. The priest welcomed them into the house, prepared a small meal. After offering grace, the priest then toasted Benjamin with wine. The day was turning out to be okay. When the boys finished eating, the priest showed the boys to their rooms for the night. It was a big house and the priest seemed to live there, all alone. Benjamin couldn't relax and slept poorly as if expecting something to happen. He couldn't explain it, but the sense of unease weighed heavily as though some kind of amorphous blob ready to pounce on him.

Morning finally came after a restless night of sleep for Benjamin. Derek, by contrast, had slept well and was determined to focus on getting back to Ottawa without dawdling any more along the way. The priest gave them a full breakfast and wished them Godspeed on their journey. Once out the door, Benjamin felt a wave of relief wash over him. With their backpacks shouldered, they walked back to the highway, put out their thumbs to passing traffic and waited.

"You boys looking for a ride?" asked the driver of a fairly new car that had stopped.

"Yeah," replied Derek. "Thanks for stopping."

"Just put your stuff in the back seat," the driver instructed. Talking to Derek he said, you sit up front with me. My name is Karl. Where are you guys headed to?"

"Ottawa," answered Benjamin as he was putting his backpack and guitar in the car while making room for himself to sit. My name is Benjamin, but almost everyone calls me Benjamin," he smiled.

"I'm Derek. Where are you heading, Karl?"

"Well, it just so happens that I'm going to Toronto. I sure wouldn't mind some company along the way. Can either of you guys drive? Have a driver's license?"

"I have a driver's license," said Derek.

"Great! I'll get you to spell me off so that we can get there sooner. How's that sound to you guys?"

"Cool! Really cool!" they said in unison.

Karl pulled back into the flow of traffic heading east passed fields of wheat and pastures filled with small poplar trees and cattle. As the hours passed, so did the towns. They stopped in Brandon for gas and a quick lunch of burgers which they ate quickly as Karl was in a hurry to continue. Though he was in a hurry, he never allowed the speedometer to exceed the speed limits, always holding it to about five miles an hour below the posted limits. Every time they saw a police car, he would slow down slightly just to make sure that they were well within the speed limit, saying, "No point in having the fuzz stop us. It'll just slow us down.

Karl and Derek switched places at Portage La Prairie. Karl watched how Derek drove for a while before he felt satisfied enough to risk sleeping. As they approached the outskirts of Winnipeg, Karl woke up and asked Derek to stop so that he could drive again. It was mid-afternoon and Karl had no intention of stopping for the day. Filling up the car, they drove on leaving the open prairie fields of wheat and corn plants, through poplar treed pastures and entered the familiar forests of spruce and pine trees.

The passing trees hypnotized with their sameness much like the constant back and forth of suspended pocket watch or the pendulum on an old grandfather clock. Karl decided to stop in Kenora for more fast food and gas. With towns being far apart along the highway in this northern forest, Karl wasn't risking running out of gas. At a smaller town called Ignace, Karl and Derek again changed places. Karl told Derek to stop at the first open gas station he saw in Fort William-Port Arthur, at the lake head.

"What do you guys say about stopping for some coffee and a bite to eat? I sure could use a break before we continue on," Karl said as he got out of the car, stretching as he tried to work out the kinks from sleeping in the car. They were at an Esso station that had a Voyageur restaurant which had its distinctive red cone atop the restaurant.

"Sound good to me," said Derek as he stretched his arms over his head, working out the tensions of holding onto the steering wheel for the past three hours.

"Me too!" Benjamin chimed in.

As they sat in the restaurant, Karl told them that they should make Marathon around midnight or so. There was a truck stop there that stayed open all night so they would be stopping there for gas and another break before heading on to Sault Ste. Marie and then the final stretch to Toronto. They stretched the break out to almost an hour before returning to the car. Karl asked Derek if he was okay to continue driving as the next leg which would be easier than the run from Marathon to Sault Ste. Marie. Agreeing to the request, Derek started the car and the journey continued.

Stopping in Marathon, only Karl got a take-out coffee. They were quickly back on the road and it didn't take long for both Benjamin and Derek to fall asleep. Karl had rested his hand on Derek's thigh. As the miles sped by, his hand found its way to Derek's crotch. Allowing his had to rest on Derek's penis for a while before daring more, a faint smile warmed Karl's face. With no negative response from Derek, Karl began to feel the shape of Derek's member which was beginning to respond to the light palpitations, a signal to Karl that Derek was okay with it, perhaps wanting even more in the silence and the darkness of the front seat.

"What the hell are you doing?" yelled Derek waking Benjamin from his sleep. "Get your hand off me!" Derek had woken up and thrust Karl's hand away in disgust and anger.

"I thought,"

"I don't care what you were thinking. Keep your effing hands to yourself, you pervert." Derek protested loudly, waking Benjamin up. "Stop the car! Let us out!"

"Easy, easy," Karl replied trying to calm Derek down."

"I said stop the car, asshole!"

"If that's what you want. But, there's nothing out there and no one is going to stop and give you a ride in this god-forsaken forest at this time of night. It would be a very long walk into Wawa. If you want, I promise that I won't touch you again, I can let you guys off in Wawa. Okay? Just don't say anything to any cops. Okay? I'm, I'm really, really sorry," Karl stuttered. "I just assumed that you two were, like, you know, homos. I'm sorry."

Derek looked a Benjamin who nodded agreement before he

turned back to Karl and said, "Okay. But if you touch me again, I'll do more than report you to the cops."

Three-quarters of an hour later, Karl left them outside of another truck stop in Wawa situated beside a seedy looking motel. Using the lights of the gas station, they found an opening in the field nearby where they set up their tents. They were both too tired and too upset to try and continue on. After trying to fall asleep without any success, Derek asked Benjamin if he would go for a coffee or something in the gas station's café. Agreeing, the boys walked the short distance to the restaurant.

"Ugh!" Derek uttered with a disgusted shaking of his whole body. "That loser was actually stroking me!"

Benjamin listened without comment to Derek as he talked through the shock of being sexually molested. Listening, was something Benjamin had learned a long time ago, intuitively knowing that it was the best way he could help.

"I don't know how to explain it," puzzled Derek. "I mean, how can you explain waking to find a man touching you, touching your privates?"

Uncharacteristically, Benjamin responded, "I know what you mean."

Looking at Benjamin, jarred by his response, Derek continued, "When I woke up it was like I was in a nightmare. I never told you, but," he hesitated undecided whether to confide a long-held secret, "When I was a kid, a priest did the same thing, touched me and stroked me."

Benjamin held his breath, not daring to say anything to interrupt.

"I was just a little kid, before I even knew you. I was in grade two. When Karl touched me, it was if I was thrown back into being a little kid, again being used. I did tell my father, but he didn't do anything about it. He blamed me for it."

As Benjamin listened, he felt lurking shadows moving around him, felt his whole being constricted leaving him struggling to breathe.

"God, there are some sick people out there!" Derek exclaimed, "And that includes my father, the prick."

Derek talked for at least another half hour before he was spent. Benjamin sat in silence, taking on Derek's pain as if it was his own. In the silence, a few tears began to well and slip down Benjamin's cheeks.

"Hey man! It's okay. The prick is gone and we're here. Let's go back to the tents and get a bit of shut- eye. We got some miles to go tomorrow."

Though they reached Sudbury without incident the next day, setting up their tents along the shore of Kelly Lake, Derek was still seething about Karl. Benjamin knew that there was nothing he could say that would make any difference. Saying anything out it at all would only make it worse for Derek. So Benjamin just made small talk while they made a simple supper of sandwiches and instant coffee. Only the passage of time would help Derek.

The next day they reached Ottawa in the late afternoon as they had a long wait in North Bay for their final ride. Their ride had left them at a shopping center in the Britannia area of the city. As they stood at a bus stop waiting for a city bus to take them into the city where they would then part with Derek heading to Hull where his parents lived and Benjamin was unsure whether he was going to stay with his grandparents or on the acreage; they agreed that they would only be staying about two weeks before they got back together for the return to Vancouver. They promised to keep in contact and perhaps get together a couple of times in the city. Derek had already phoned home and his father was going to pick him up downtown. Benjamin had tried to phone his grandparents, but there wasn't an answer. He decided to try later when they got downtown.

Chapter Thirteen

"Hello?"

Benjamin was surprised to hear his father's voice answer the phone. "Hi, Dad, It's Benjamin."

"Benjamin?" There was the sound of pleased surprise in his father's voice. "Where are you?"

"I'm in the city. I just got in. I just went to Mémère's and Pépère's but they aren't there anymore."

"They moved to Lower Town. Pépère couldn't do the maintenance work anymore. Are you going to come home?" Laurent asked with what sounded like a hint of hope.

"I didn't know if I could," Benjamin explained. "Mom threw me out."

"Come home, son. Catch the bus and I'll pick you up at the Alta Vista shopping center, okay?"

"Sure, Dad." Benjamin said with a hint of doubt. His father had often left him hanging after making arrangements before, always saying that something important had come up and that there wasn't any way to let Benjamin know about it. "Are you sure it's okay with Mom?"

"Here she is, she'll tell you herself." Benjamin couldn't believe the sense of joy he had heard in his father's voice. Perhaps it was real.

"Hi, Benny," said his mother on the phone.

"Hi Mom. Is it okay with you that I come to the farm?"

"Of course!" she exclaimed. "Why wouldn't it be okay?"

"Um, you told me never to come back."

"I did? I don't remember ever saying that. It's probably your over active imagination again. Dad is outside starting the car. He'll pick you up," Betsy added cheerfully. "See you soon, Benny. The kids will be so excited to see you."

When he got off the bus at the shopping center, his father was already there, waiting for him as he had promised. Laurent got out of the car and gave his son a big hug followed by a pat on the back. Benjamin couldn't believe it as the last time they had been together at Kevin's birthday party, it had ended up with Benjamin throwing a punch at him. What had changed? Whatever it was, Benjamin was grateful for the change, he hugged his father back and began to tear up at the edges of his eyes.

"Put your stuff in the back. Let's go home."

"Are you home for good?" Laurent asked as they drove off.

"No, Dad, just for two weeks. I have to head back to my job in Vancouver."

"A job in Vancouver? What kind of job?"

"I'm a stock auditor and deal with inventory control for stores." Benjamin explained without going into a lot of detail.

"You always were good at Math. Pay's good?"

"Yeah. Pretty good," Benjamin confirmed without saying how much he earned. His senses were now on high alert. When money was involved, he always found himself guilted into giving almost everything he earned to his parents.

"I have a new job," his father told him. "I am building houses. Your brothers Georges and Gordon are helping during the summer. Your uncles, Blaise and Bernard are also working with me. I was hoping that you would maybe work with me, Benjamin. We could be partners."

"No, Dad. I got a good job and I like it. Thanks for asking though."

"That's okay. I don't blame you. I guess I haven't been the best of father's."

"It's not that Dad. It's just that I really do like my job. And, I love living in BC."

Laurent turned and looked at his son. "You've grown up Benjamin, become a man. It's good to see, son." Then he grinned and commented with a laugh, "Your mother sure isn't going to like the hair and your beard."

As the car pulled into the graveled driveway, most of Benjamin's brothers and sisters were rushing to the car to greet Benjamin, with Gordon, Suzanne and Neil leading the group. Béatrice and Georges held back waiting by the door. Gordon struggled to carry the backpack and Neil pleaded, asking if he could carry the guitar. Justin helped by putting his hand of the bottom of the guitar case as they bumped their way to the house. Only his mother wasn't in the yard to greet him, and of course Kevin who was somewhere with the army he had joined.

As Benjamin neared the door to the house, Georges stepped forward and greeted him with a firm grip and a smile. Béatrice was carrying Heather who was now two years old and smiled as she said, "Hi Benjamin." Entering the house, he saw that the dining room table was set with a bowl of spaghetti sauce sitting in the center of it. His mother had cooked spaghetti, a meal that everyone was Benjamin's favorite.

"You look so scruffy with that beard, and you need a haircut, you look like a hoodlum with all that hair! Here, give your mother a kiss," Betsy complained as she put her cheek out for the expected kiss. "Just leave your bag in the entry for now. We'll figure out where you'll sleep after supper."

"Yes, Mom."

"Okay, everyone to the table. It's supper time."

The meal was noisy and filled with laughter. Benjamin answered questions between mouthfuls of spaghetti, making sure that he found something funny to add to each of his answers. At one point, he ended up describing being on the ferry during a strong wind with people getting seasick and how they screamed with each huge wave tossing the ferry. When the meal was done, Benjamin took out his guitar and sang some of the new songs he had learned while he had been away. Finally, his mother told Béatrice to put Heather and Justin to bed and then do the supper dishes.

"You'll have to bunk in with Georges until Béatrice can clean her stuff out of your room. Tomorrow you'll get a haircut and a shave. You can't work with your father with all that hair. It's not safe. You'll go to work with him the next day," Betsy told Benjamin.

"Béatrice can keep the room. I'll just sleep on the sofa," replied Benjamin. "And no, I'm not going to work with Dad. Gordon and Georges. And no, I'm not getting my haircut. I'm going to visit Mémère and Pépère tomorrow."

"You can visit them on Sunday. You can't just sit around like you're on holidays," she continued.

"But I am on holidays, Mom. I go back to work in two weeks," Benjamin told her realizing that he hadn't told her yet because of all the excitement and fuss.

"Don't you know your Dad needs you?" she said with a hint of anger in her voice. "Georges can only help so much, and Gordon is almost useless as a helper. You don't want him to lose the contract and money, do you?"

"Mom, I came to visit, not to move back. I'm not coming back home to live."

"Why are you always so selfish? All you do is think of yourself. Can't you see that we need help here?"

Benjamin just shook his head. All the good feelings that had been building up since his arrival began to evaporate. Thinking that life at home had somehow magically transformed with the return of his father was too much to hope for. His mother was still all about herself, still angry. She only showed nice when there was something to gain from it. The news that he was going to be leaving and not staying and giving her a significant part of his salary was enough to bring back her dark side.

"Betsy," interjected his father. "He just got home. Enough!"

"Yes, Lou," she said with her meek voice not wanting to bring on his anger.

Laurent dropped Benjamin off at the shopping center and then continued on to the construction work site with Georges. Benjamin promised to come back to the farm house later the same day after his visit to his grandparents'. He told his father not to worry about picking him up at the shopping center as he would make his own way to the farm and would likely get there before they did.

It was too early for him to go to his grandparents' place, so Benjamin decided to wander along Sparks Street Mall and then walk to the Bytown Market for a coffee. Sitting at an outside table with his coffee, he reminisced about the past when he had gone to the market with his grandparents. He remembered maple sugar candy and toffee which would be made in a bed of snow. There were good times in the past. Another memory of shopping for a Thanksgiving turkey with his grandmother floated into his consciousness. Swallowing the last of his coffee, he thanked the waitress and made his way the remaining three blocks.

"Oh, Mon Dieu!" exclaimed his grandmother. "C'est Jésus Christ!"

With a grin, Benjamin wrapped his arms around his grandmother in a hug as he said, "Non, Mémère, c'est moi, Benjamin!"

She put her hands on his cheeks and gave him a big kiss and then called out to his grandfather, "Gilles, Benjamin s'en venue."

Benjamin spent the rest of the morning with his grandparents, had lunch with them and part of the afternoon. He told them about his job and life in British Columbia, making sure that what he told them was positive. Asking about the extended family, they told him about his aunts, uncles and cousins who were almost as close as his brothers and sisters. Her youngest two were more like older brothers than uncles. There was none of the formality that was the norm when Benjamin was with his mother's family, his English relatives. As Benjamin prepared to leave, he promised his grandparents that he would be back again, soon.

Benjamin then returned to the Alta Vista shopping center where he stopped long enough to buy a bottle of orange juice to drink before heading out to hitch a ride to the farm house. Standing on the road, it was almost as if he had never left. It was all so familiar, so normal. Yet, there was a difference. The difference was in him. He had changed and he felt it. The dread of going home wasn't near as strong as it used to be. It was as if he had somehow grown a protective layer that would keep the bad stuff away.

The next few days passed with Benjamin taking time to visit various cousins, aunts and uncles, as well as spending time working in the large yard at home cutting grass and cleaning us some of the boards that had fallen off the old barn at the back of the yard. Benjamin also did his part helping around the house. He played music and even took some time to teach Neil a little guitar, a few basic chords. Every time that Benjamin would take out his guitar to practice or to entertain his brothers and sisters, Neil was sure to take the old guitar that had been left for him when Benjamin had to leave last December, and strum the strings. Gordon was usually gone to the worksite with his brother and father. At twelve, he was a helpful pair of arms, someone who would be sent for a tool or asked to hold a board while it was cut. Benjamin's father paid Gordon a small amount which somehow seemed to be a lot of money to him.

Laurent had remained living at the house, returning every evening with the boys. When he was home, Betsy became a smiling person; she would make a fuss over the meal and over her husband. The contrast with her personality when his father was at work and when he was at home was staggering. Almost as soon as his father went out the door, her face took on an angry bitterness as she pinched and twisted the ears of Béatrice and Suzanne, who at nine years of age, was considered old enough to do her fair share of the housework.

Of course, his mother was exempt from any of the work. She either sat or brooded in the dining room where she could continually hound the girls, or sat in front of the television watching her favorite programs and drinking tea, or she disappeared into her room to read magazines. Neil and Justin played outside unsupervised as often as they could, and sat in front of the television the rest of the time. Heather sometimes was always with her brothers watching television or playing outside with them.

Benjamin felt a burden of sadness as he saw how life was unfolding for his brothers and sisters. The only time his mother acted even a little bit like a mother was when her husband was in the house. Most of the days that he returned from visiting in the city, he would find Béatrice had gone out leaving Suzanne to face their mother's anger. Benjamin helped Suzanne without being asked to do so, doing dishes and laundry while Suzanne tried her best to sweep and tidy up.

The last phone call to Derek had upset Benjamin. They had only been back six days and already there had been a fight between Derek and his father. Derek had phoned Benjamin to tell him that he was leaving the city to stay with some cousins in Kingston. Derek suggested that they could meet up there when Benjamin was ready to head back.

Benjamin decided that he would leave the following Sunday, the first Sunday of August. It shortened the time he had thought he would spend in Ottawa by a week; however, he was anxious to go back to Vancouver, see Jacqueline and his aunt and uncle. Benjamin also wanted to get back and get more involved in the folk music scene there. With luck, perhaps he could even make a career out of music. But mostly, he wanted to get away from the ghosts that lurked in the shadows of the house, and the anger and bitterness of his mother. The only thing he would regret was leaving his brothers and sisters to have to deal with that anger and bitterness. If he stayed, he could protect them. But he knew that to stay would also be the worst thing he could do.

At nights, when everyone was sleeping in the house, Benjamin had found himself sitting in the living room listening to classical music on the radio which was put on as low a volume as possible while letting him still here it. He sat in the darkness. He had tried sleeping, but the silence seemed to invite old ghosts to torment him. The idea of leaving a week early gave him enough energy to go through the final days without incident.

It was Sunday, and Benjamin was gathering his stuff together, packing them in his backpack while a few of his brother's watched. Benjamin had already told them that he would return the next summer when he got holidays again. Gordon was wondering if maybe Benjamin could bring him a pair of cowboy boots for him, and maybe a cowboy hat, too. Without thinking about it, Benjamin picked out his suede jacket and boots telling Gordon to try on the boots. Calling Georges, he told him to try on the jacket.

The boots were big on Gordon, but not so big as to be too hard to walk in. While Gordon still had on the cowboy boots, Benjamin told him "They fit you perfectly! How about these? They're used. Are they good enough?"

Gordon was speechless, his mouth hanging open in surprise. Finally he asked with a bit of apprehension, "You mean, it Benny? You mean I can have these?" As Benjamin nodded his head while grinning, Gordon gave a whoop and ran off to show Suzanne his new treasure.

Benjamin turned to Georges and saw that the jacket was a good fit and that it looked good on him. "Well, Georges," he said, "It's yours if you want it." With his characteristic quietness, Georges hugged his older brother and said thanks. The look in Georges' eyes confirmed for Benjamin that it had been a wise decision. His brother's eyes said it all.

Benjamin had accumulated a parting gift for each of his brothers and sisters over the past week knowing that he was leaving them. Choosing each gift was hard, very hard. It almost felt as if the gift was a copout from giving them what they needed most, him. He had also bought his mother and father a small gift.

"You think this is going to pay for all the food you ate?" complained his mother when Benjamin gave her an original Royal Dolton cup and saucer, an expensive gift in comparison to all the other gifts he had purchased.

Benjamin had been prepared for just this kind of response as he pulled out an envelope with half of his remaining money within it.

"I hope this covers the bill. I didn't expect that it was enough just being your son." Benjamin knew that what he had said was mean, but his mother didn't seem to hear as she was too focused on counting out the contents in the envelope.

"Is this all?" snarled his mother after noticing that Benjamin hadn't given her even more of the money from his wallet.

Picking up his backpack, and giving each of his brothers and sisters a final hug, he followed his father out of the door. Laurent was going to drive him to the shopping center from where Benjamin would then make his way out of the city and on to hopefully reach Kingston that same day.

As Benjamin reached into the back seat to get his backpack his father said, "Benjamin, this is your birthday gift." His father was holding out an Esso credit card, one that was being used for his house construction business. "Don't worry about anything. I'll pay for whatever you use it for." And then, Laurent hugged his eldest son before turning away and walking back into the house.

Surprised and speechless, Benjamin could only look up at his father with surprise. "Travel safe and for Pete's sake, call us every once in a while, son."

"Thanks, Dad. I will call," were the only words he could find to speak to his father. "I guess I'd better go," he added after a moment of confused silence. "See you, Dad."

Chapter Fourteen

Turning the corner onto Anderson Road, Benjamin soon caught a ride into Carlsbad Springs and highway 41. He didn't wait long for his next ride which took him all the way to Smith Falls, where he stopped for a Fudgsicle and a Coke, before catching another ride to Kingston. Benjamin had arranged to meet Derek at the Lemoine Conservation Area where he would be waiting at the Rotary Park. The journey took him just over four hours even though it was less than a hundred and twenty miles to travel from Ottawa to Kingston.

It was mid-afternoon and still quite warm when Benjamin had finally set up his tent in the park next to Derek's tent. The guys decided that a good swim was needed in order to cool off. Benjamin had picked up his old bathing suit while at the house when he was packing up, so there was no problem on that count. Soon the boys found themselves at the pool jumping off the ten foot diving board, doing cannon balls and the occasional mistimed back flop. They left the pool cheerfully, while good-naturedly complaining of their aches and pains suffered from the high diving board. Feeling hungry after the exercise, they decided to eat at the park's small café rather than cook themselves up a camp meal.

After returning to the tent for the rest of the evening, they built a small camp fire and sat around it taking turns talking of their Ottawa experiences. Usually, it was Derek who did most of the talking. However, this time, he had little to say and what he did say was more about people and places while avoiding talking about his parents. The plan for the next day was to go as far west as possible, hoping that they could get as far as Sudbury, if not further.

They packed up early the next morning and soon found

themselves standing on the highway that would take them west to Toronto from where they would then head north on highway sixty-nine to Sudbury. They stood on the edge of the highway watching as car after car passed without slowing down. The long wait for a ride soon had them wilting in the heat. Finally after almost two hours, a car stopped to give them a ride into the city of Toronto. The man driving the car was named Donald. He was young, not more than two years older than them. As he drove west, he was telling the boys about his home in Etobicoke. Apparently he was living there alone for the summer, while his parents were off touring somewhere in Europe.

Derek told Donald about their hoped for destination for the night, wondering if Donald could drop them off on the right highway north. It was already afternoon as they were making their way through the heavy summer traffic that congested the city. Since it was too late in the day to think about getting a ride towards Sudbury, Donald offered to let them stay in his house for the night. He told them that he would take them to the highway the next morning. Since offers such as this were typical and not unexpected, Derek and Benjamin agreed to stay the night.

The house in Etobicoke was near the shore of Lake Ontario, no more than two blocks away. The house was quite modern and rather large. Benjamin could tell that it was a very expensive home. Donald's parents had covered most of the furniture with clear plastic sheets in order to keep the dust off of them. Only the rooms that Donald had need of were not filled with plastic. Donald showed them where they could sleep in the basement, a guest room. They could have separate rooms with a shared bathroom just down the hall. Donald suggested they put their stuff in their rooms for the night and then come up to the back kitchen for a late lunch and some coffee or whatever to drink. The boys couldn't believe their luck. This was the nicest place they had been in for a long time. It was even nicer than Ben and Jennie's upscale apartment in Vancouver.

Donald was a good host, perhaps too good. As they sat around the small kitchen just off the back garden, Donald offered them home-made cigarettes. Derek being a smoker readily accepted and lit up the cigarette using the same match that Donald used to light his. It took Benjamin only a few moments to realize that the cigarettes were joints. Benjamin knew the smell of marijuana, having had school friends and then work mates in Ottawa who regularly toked up. Some of those people had been caught and were now in jail. It was obvious that Derek also knew as he commented with a grin that it was good shit. Benjamin had never smoked weed before and was not ready to begin smoking dope.

"Jeez, man," Derek complained. "A toke isn't going to kill you."

Benjamin refused to take the toke leaving Derek to just shrug his shoulders as if to say, 'Your loss.' Donald held out a large bag of marijuana and opened up his cigarette package to show them that it was almost filled with marijuana cigarettes already rolled and ready for smoking.

"You guys want to stay here longer and help me smoke this shit?"

They were still there three days later. Derek was frequently out with Donald during that time while Benjamin sat in the yard or in the kitchen playing his guitar, or listening to the radio. He also went for walks along the lakeshore. Benjamin suspected that Derek and Donald were drinking, and perhaps even finding a few unscrupulous women to screw. The signals were all there: the smells and the satisfied looks on their faces when they returned.On that Wednesday afternoon, while listening to the radio, Benjamin heard the announcer talking about a music festival that was to happen that weekend at Mosport Freeway, something they called Strawberry Fields, Canada's answer to Woodstock, a festival that had taken place the previous summer in the States. The announcer mentioned that the festival was organized by John Lennon and Yoko Ono. It seemed that the festival had originally been set for a location in New Brunswick and was only now, at the last minute being set up just north of the city. Benjamin wanted to go to the festival and hoped he could persuade Derek to leave the house and go to the festival and then travel on back to Vancouver. Benjamin decided to bring up the topic later that afternoon before Derek got too stoned again.

"Hell, yes!" answered Derek. "It'll be a three-day party. What do you think, Donald? Game for it?"

Benjamin hadn't counted on Derek inviting Donald, but it was too late to change it now. At least he was leaving the city. Hopefully he could convince Derek to head to Vancouver from the festival on Monday when the concert was over. If not, he would go back on his own.

~

As Donald drove in through the gates into the Mosport Freeway Race Track grounds and found a place to park, the three young men saw that the radio had not been exaggerating the numbers of people at the site. If anything, it seemed they had under-estimated. There had to be almost a hundred thousand people there instead of the predicted fifty thousand. It seemed that the number of people in line behind them would soon take that number a lot higher. They had each paid their fifteen dollars at the gate and walked down a dirt road to the camping area. They had planned on being early so as to have their tents set up near the stage where the musicians would be playing. With almost five hours to go before the first act would appear on stage, they saw that there was no way they could get a close site. The got as close as possible and left Benjamin to set up the two pup tents while Derek went back with Donald to get the larger tent that Donald was going to use. It wasn't long before all was set. They had time to kill and a lot to discover while waiting.

As they walked around the grounds they passed a group of about fifteen naked young men and women splashing at the edge of a dugout. Derek snickered and told Donald that they should go back to the dugout and join the nudies. Benjamin shook his head. He just couldn't understand what was happening to his friend. Over the past few days, Derek was so totally out of it, that Benjamin was beginning to think he would have to take him to a psych ward, the same as he did with Céline. He wasn't yet aware of the fact that both Donald and Derek had been swallowing tabs of LSD, acid. It wasn't long before Derek and Donald decided it was time to take a time-out for a joint or two.

Benjamin stuffed his backpack into the back of the tent, took his guitar and went wandering around the site hoping to find a good spot to watch the performances that evening. He spotted a group of four young people, two guys and girls, who were all playing guitars together. As they noticed him, they called him over and encouraged Benjamin to join in on the jam session. They played for more than an hour. As they took a short break and talked about the music to come with performances by Luke and the Apostles and Feliciano, one of the girls began taking off her clothes saying how hot she was. It was hot, very hot. And so when she challenged them to do the same, saying it was time to get real the rest of the group soon found themselves naked.

With their clothing in a heap, and again playing their guitars, a bigger crowd of listeners gathered some of them stripping off their clothes and then dancing to the rhythms. Someone was passing out glasses of Kool-Aid and bottles of water. Benjamin hated Kool-Aid, as it reminded him too much of poverty, and happily accepted water to quench his thirst. After another hour, he found himself the only one still playing. The others had stopped and were now swaying as though hypnotized by the music that could barely be heard for the increasing noise of the festival crowd. There was little doubt that the Kool-aid had been spiked with LSD.

Benjamin decided it was time to head back to the tent and make himself a bite to eat as he was hungry. He hadn't eaten anything since breakfast time. The groceries were in Donald's tent so Benjamin shouted out, "knock, knock" before entering. Not hearing anything, he walked in and saw Derek passed out in the tent with a skinny, long-haired girl who couldn't have been fourteen years old sitting dazed beside him. Both were nude. Surprised at the sight, he suddenly became aware that he had forgotten his clothes where they had fallen while he had been playing with the others a few hours earlier. How hadn't anyone noticed and commented on it to him as he walked back to his tent nude and carrying his guitar? Grabbing a loaf of bread and a bag of chips which he tossed into his little tent; and then putting on a pair of shorts, he left and went looking for his lost clothes.

Benjamin was still wandering around, still in search of his clothes, when the music started playing. There were too many people around for him to locate the place he had been playing with the others. It began to seem a hopeless task. While walking, searching the ground for his clothes, he passed by a quite a few Volkswagen minivans decorated with swirls of color and paisley flowers, and all the colors of the rainbow; he passed old buses, small circus tents and thousands upon thousands of people simply sitting or lying on the ground. He knew he would never find his clothes, and that he should just give them up as lost. After all, he had only lost a pair of cut-off jeans and an old tee-shirt.

He tried to retrace his steps, looking for the landmarks he had made during the search. He was surprised more than once seeing people making out on the ground, oblivious of the people standing around them, some of them watching them as if at a show. People selling weed in vans with their doors opened for all passersby to see the joints, water pipes, hash pipes as well as roach clips and more. Some were selling more booze that he had ever seen in one place. Everything was in plain sight with no fear of police and arrests.

Though the sun was setting, the heat was still almost unbearable in this swarm of bodies that were in constant motion. It was relief when Benjamin finally reached his tent. There was no way he was going to move from the spot until noise and swell of bodies came to a rest. He also realized that he didn't need to get any closer to the stage. He actually could see the stage from where he was sitting, though the people on the stage were not very big or even recognizable. More importantly, the sound system ensured that he could hear the music over the constant hum. He had already eaten the chips and was still hungry, so he decided to eat some of the bread with peanut butter, the only sandwich filler he had brought along. He searched in Derek's empty tent and found a couple of bottles of Coke and took one of them. It would have to do for the night as that was all there was to drink. He definitely wasn't going back into Donald's tent to get something out of the two coolers of food and drink that they had brought with them.

Benjamin woke up late the next morning. He had only slept about five or six hours, but the tent felt like a sauna. Crawling out of the tent, he saw that there were still people arriving at the festival site. Benjamin felt grubby and sticky and he needed a shower. However, there wasn't any chance that he'd find a shower on the grounds. Remembering the dugout that he had seen when they arrived the day before, Benjamin thought it would be good enough. At least it was wet and would cool him off. Taking a towel out of his backpack, he walked towards the entrance where he had seen the dugout. It was impossible to walk in a straight line to get to the entrance road as the tents, vans, and scattered cars weren't parked or set up in any kind of order. As well, many had simply spent the night in sleeping bags on the ground in whatever spaces they could find. Even though so many were sleeping, he could hear the noise of incoming traffic and excited voices.

There were others who had also woken up and were sleepily wandering in search of toilets or perhaps friends they had lost sometime during the party that had gone on until the first hint of dawn. Reaching the road, the way became easier. There were still cars and vans coming into the grounds having to drive to the distant edges of the festival site in search of a place to park themselves for Saturday's festival program. Benjamin spotted the dugout and saw that he wasn't going to be the first into the water. There had to be at least two dozen people already splashing at the edges of the pond. Like the day before, all were stark naked.

Benjamin was careful in choosing a place to put his towel and shorts before joining the others in the pond. He stood on the edges with his feet in the water for a few moments before he walked further into the pond, making his way towards the center where he could hopefully swim. Benjamin reached a spot where it was deep enough to totally submerge himself and then swim a bit, mostly treading water and feeling the water move across his body. He was a comfortable distance from the others and was able to watch them while he moved slowly through the center of the pond. He hadn't brought any shampoo or soap and began to wonder if he could share a bar of soap that was being passed around on the edge of the pond. The idea was enough to have Benjamin bridge the distance and then hold out his hand as though he was next in line for its use.

A young woman with long, dark brown hair and a dark complexion saw his hand reaching for the soap. Giving Benjamin a smile, she simply said "Peace, Man," as she passed it on. He quickly soaped under his arms, his genitals and then his hair so that he could pass the bar of soap on to another guy who was waiting his turn.

After almost an hour in the pond, Benjamin climbed back onto the shore and retrieved his towel. The air was more than warm enough with a breeze to dry his body, so he just toweled his hair. Standing there, not self-conscious of his nudity, he folded up his towel and placed it on the ground for something to sit on when the girl who had passed him the bar of soap asked if she could use the towel to dry her hair as well. Benjamin was quick to give her the towel and watched her use it. He couldn't help but notice the thatch of black hair that hid her vagina and the dark aureoles that surrounded the nipples of her full, young breasts. She saw him looking and smiled. Then, handing him the towel, she walked off to join up with her group. As they left the pond area, she turned back, gave Benjamin another smile and a wave of her hand.

Benjamin turned back to look at the others who were still in the pond and to sit. There wasn't any rush to get back to the tent. Besides, he would likely want to go into the water again simply to cool off before heading back for something to eat. As he watched, he noticed how there was no one making out. He wondered about it after having seen people unabashedly making out the evening before on the grounds, wondered why there was a difference. The scene was as innocent as one would find at a normal swimming pool with people simply having fun in the water. Maybe, he thought, it was because they weren't stoned or drunk. They were simply young people having a good time.

Hunger pangs told him it was time to head back to the tent and get himself something to eat. Once back, there was still no sign of Derek or Donald. Benjamin went into the larger tent, opened up the cooler and took out a carton of juice and broke off a hunk of cheese. The cooler was still full of most of the stuff they had brought to the site. Taking the food and juice out of the tent, he returned to the front of his tent, sat down and ate while waiting for another day of music to begin.

Derek sat beside Benjamin late Sunday evening. Derek had surfaced that morning and had spent most of the day in his own tent, sleeping. Benjamin had just returned from his second visit to the pond when Derek showed up. Donald was nowhere to be seen as he hadn't appeared back at the tent during the past two days. Benjamin passed Derek a cheese sandwich and a Coke and sat back sipping on a 7 Up.

"You ready to leave, Derek? You going to go back to Vancouver with me? I'm leaving first thing in the morning."

"Yeah," he replied. "Man, am I ever wasted. God, does my head hurt."

Benjamin had little sympathy for his best friend, perhaps his only friend. "Booze and drugs – not such a good combination, huh?"

"Yeah, I know," he answered. "Hey, that voice sounds familiar! Who's playing?"

Benjamin answered, "Jose Féliciano."

"Jeez, he's good."

"So what was with you and Donald, Derek, where have you been?"

"Money, hot chicks, booze, LSD – I just wanted it all. Shit, Benjamin, I just wanted to wipe out everything in my head, make it empty."

"Doesn't work, does it?"

"Nah – the shit's still there. Nothing makes it go away."

"I know. Believe me, I know," confirmed Benjamin.

The two boys sat silent listening to the music all night until the sun was about to rise when Sly and the Family Stone finished their last song bringing the festival to an end. They hadn't slept all night, but they decided to pack up and leave before the big crowd decided to get moving and make leaving a nightmare of a traffic jam. They couldn't imagine trying to work their way to the exit if all two hundred and fifty thousand of the festival goers were to try leaving at the same time.

Once through to the road, they made their way, walking through the parking lot and onto Highway 20. They managed to catch a ride with one of the first vehicles leaving the parking lot which took them to a small town called Brooklin on Highway 7, where they stopped for breakfast, the first decent meal since breakfast three days earlier. With breakfast done, they headed back to the highway and soon caught a ride to the junction of Highway 27.

The next ride was a lot longer in coming, a ride that took them all the way to Sudbury and the Trans- Canada Highway. It was late afternoon by the time they arrived in Sudbury, but still they continued hitch- hiking, pushing to put as much distance as possible between them and the ghosts that haunted them in the east. The boys did get a final ride, a short one, to Espanola. Before they called it a day and set up their tent.

The next morning they caught a ride that took them all the way to Nipigon and then a second ride into Thunder Bay where they stayed the night. It was raining the next morning as they stood on the highway hitch-hiking. They were there for over an hour when a young man stopped and told them he was taking them home with him for coffee and a chance to dry out. It was supposed to stop raining in the afternoon and he promised to bring them back to the highway when it stopped raining. Benjamin looked at Derek and suggested that this time, it probably was an honest offer. So they accepted the ride and were surprised when the young man's wife was there with hot coffee waiting for them.

"We saw you when we were coming back from the grocery store," she told them. "When I sent, Bill here, back out to get something we forgotten to buy, he told me that you were still out there in the rain, so I sent him back to get the two of you. Here, have some coffee. I hope you have a change of clothes to wear while we put those ones in the dryer. If not, Bill will lend you something to wear until they are ready."

They were back on the highway by two in the afternoon. As promised, the rain had stopped enough to make hitch-hiking worth attempting. If they were still there at supper time, Bill would return and pick them up. They made it to Falcon Lake, Manitoba and stopped at the campgrounds there for the rest of the day. The next morning it was a three-ride day taking them as far as Brandon, Manitoba. They decided it was worth the time to have a decent meal at the Voyageur Restaurant where they had been dropped off. Benjamin decided he may as well see if the Esso credit card his father had given him would be accepted. If not, he still had enough money to pay for his food. He was surprised when the credit card was returned saying that the bill had been paid, that the card was indeed good.

It was slower going on the prairies as people were less willing to pick up hitchhikers. From Brandon, they caught a ride that took them all the way to Medicine Hat, Alberta. The boys were tired from the constant, focused work of hitch-hiking and needed a day's rest. Medicine Hat seemed to be the perfect spot for a pause. It was big enough to avoid being a target for rednecks out to get hippies, yet not so big as to be a concrete jungle. They found a campground not too far from the old downtown area near the river and set up there, planning on spending two nights there. Then, they walked into the downtown and found a decent restaurant selling country breakfasts all day long. Bacon, eggs, hash browns and thick slices of toast made a hearty supper that was well appreciated. Derek suggested going for a beer, promising it would only be one beer, before they returned to the campsite and their tents.

When they packed up after their rest day, they only needed two rides to make it as far as Revelstoke, BC. Another night at another campground and they were on the road early hoping to make it to Vancouver.

They had barely put out their thumbs when a car stopped for them. They made it into the city by mid- afternoon. They had finished their summer journey. They had been gone more than six weeks and were looking forward to getting to Jacqueline's place and resuming the good life. Besides, their money was almost all spent. With luck, they could make it to their first paycheck before their money ran out, assuming Doug had work for them as he had suggested in June, a start back with the start of September.

Chapter Fifteen

Getting off the city bus a block from Jacqueline's Benjamin began to wonder if they should have phoned first. What if no one was at the basement suite? What if she had moved? Benjamin remembered that he had promised to return in three weeks; and now, six weeks later, here he was not having phoned even once, would she want them back? Derek hadn't seemed too worried about it as Jacqueline had been living in the suite for almost two years since she had left her parent's home. He thought it extremely unlikely that she would move; after all, the plan to keep the team together for the next set of road trips had still been the plan when they left for Ottawa. As they walked the path into the backyard where the door to the suite was located, they saw that only the screen door was closed. With the main door open, they knew that someone was at home. The only question was, was it Jacqueline? Before entering, they knocked on the screen door and called out.

"Who are you?" asked a man who appeared to be in his late twenties who stood barring the way into the suite. "You can't just walk into someone's house without permission."

"I'm sorry," apologized Benjamin, "I thought, we thought," apologizing as he pointed to Derek and then himself, "that our friend lived here."

Hearing Benjamin's voice, Jacqueline appeared from out of the bedroom saying, "Is that you, Benjamin?" before she turned and saw Derek. "You came back?" she uttered in surprise. "I thought that you guys were never coming back. You said three weeks. I assumed that once you guys were back home, you decided to stay there."

"Hi Jacqueline," both boys spoke at the same time. Benjamin

continued, "I'm sorry, Jacqueline. I know we should've called, but somehow I just assumed,"

Benjamin walked further into the kitchen in order to give her a big hug when Jack interrupted, "Whoa, there. I still don't have a frigging clue who you guys are. And, there's no way you're going to put your paws on my woman."

Benjamin came to an abrupt halt just as he was about to give Jacqueline a hug. He looked at her then at Jack and mumbled, "Boyfriend?"

"Jack," soothed Jacqueline in an attempt to diffuse his aggressiveness, "these are my old workmates, Derek and Benjamin. You know, the inventory guys. They stayed with me for a couple of weeks after the summer shut down began before they headed home. You remember, I told you about them?"

"Yeah, now I remember," Jack admitted as he began to relax. "I'm Jack by the way," he said as he continued. Pointing to Benjamin, he said, "You must be Benjamin, the short skinny one."

"Yes, I'm Benjamin and this is Derek," he said with a touch of relief now that Jack had unclenched his fists.

"Benjamin, I told you we should have called before coming here," Derek interjected happy for once that it was Benjamin and not him who the others thought had screwed up.

"So what do you guys want?" asked Jack with some residual tension lingering on the edges of his voice.

"We were hoping we could stay with Jacqueline until work started," answered Derek. "That had been the plan when we left."

"No can do," replied Jack. "You guys are outta luck." Holding out his hand indicating that it was time to leave, he continued," Nice meeting you guys. Maybe we'll see you around another time."

Derek took Jack's hand and said "Nice meeting you too." Realizing that they had just been told to leave, Benjamin turned away and began walking towards the door they had just entered.

Jacqueline interjected. "Jack! These my friends and this is my place! Of course they can stay for a few days until they get their own place."

Jack's face turned a dark red as he looked back at Jacqueline, "Your place, huh," before storming off to the bedroom. Only to re-emerge with his jacket and runners. "I'll be back. And, I don't want these guys here when I return." Then he walked out in a huff, slamming the screen door behind him.

"I'm sorry, guys," Jacqueline apologized. "Jack doesn't like surprises. He's actually a nice guy, just a little insecure when it comes to other people, especially guy people."

"It's okay," Benjamin muttered apologetically, "We understand. We'll just set up our tents in the park for now. No sweat. You don't have to apologize. We should've phoned first."

"No, it's okay. You guys can stay here for a few days. Don't worry about Jack. He'll be cool," promised Jacqueline. "Just one thing, keep your clothes on and don't bring any girls, and stay out of our room."

They stayed four days. Jack had indeed calmed down and decided that Derek was his new best friend. Derek and

Benjamin saw little of either Jack or Jacqueline when Jack wasn't at work as they stayed in the bedroom for the most part. The smell of unwashed sex was strong each time one of them left the room to go to the bathroom or to the kitchen for some food. The few times they did come out of the bedroom together, it was about the music which Benjamin was playing. Jack shared his stash of hash with Derek and Jacqueline while Benjamin played. Benjamin refused to take his turn at the pipe being passed around.

On the third day, Benjamin and Derek went to the office in search of Doug only to find out that Doug was away with a crew on the Sunshine Coast. He was expected back after the September long week-end. When they asked about their own return to work, all they were told was to ask Doug when he was back.

"Derek," Benjamin said the next evening while Jack and Jacqueline were again ensconced in the bedroom, the noise of their love-making sounding through the thin walls, "Let's leave. I'm not comfortable being here. Let's go camping on the Island. We'll come back after the long week-end and see Doug about work. What do you say?"

"Sure, why not?" he answered. "We could always head to Denman and Hornby Islands. I just read in the paper that it is a happening place right now. It could be fun. Hornby's got this famous hippy beach that we could camp on."

Packing up their stuff, they slipped out of the house while Jack and Jacqueline were still in the bedroom which had now gone quiet. Likely they were asleep for a while. Before leaving, Benjamin left Jacqueline a note telling her where they were going and when they would be back. She already knew about Doug not being in the city until after the long week-end. She had told the boys that they would go see Doug together about going back to work.

They took the bus towards the Horseshoe Bay Ferry rather than to cross to the Island on the Tsawwassen Ferry. Getting off at Nanaimo would cut the distance to Denman and Hornby Islands by quite a bit. With luck, they would be setting up their tents on Hornby Island later that afternoon. It was a sunny day and it felt good to be moving again. Sitting in the darkened basement suite for the past few days had been depressing, especially given the situation with Jacqueline and Jack. Somehow, the addition of Jack had signaled an end to the harmony of the group of five that had built up over the six months of working together and living together for the most part.

The ferry ride to Departure Bay was uneventful, which was likely a good thing, as Benjamin stood at the railing for most of the ferry trip, staring at the water. He only went in once to buy a cup of coffee. Derek had been wandering around as usual, unable to sit still and just relax. Benjamin wondered how it was that someone so different from himself could be his best friend. But, for most of the ride, he didn't think of anything at all as he stared at the water.

The booming horn of the ferry brought him back to the present, back to reality as they prepared to dock. They were off early enough to catch one of the cars heading north along the Island Highway. The ride that took them as far as Parksville. They had a wait of almost an hour before another car stopped. Since the driver was headed to Courtney, they made arrangements to get off at the exit for Denman Island in order to catch the first of two small ferries to reach Hornby Island. Being that they were foot passengers, they didn't have to worry about waiting in the long line up of cars that would have meant a delay of two hours. They easily caught a ride to the next ferry and were crossing over to Hornby with plenty of time left in the day for finding a campsite and setting up their tents.

"No campsites on Hornby," the driver of the last car, a woman in her late thirties told them. "The cops were in a few days ago and the bulldozed everything down chasing the hippies off who had been camped there for the past few months."

"Is there any other place we can set up our tents for the week-end?" asked Derek.

"There's just the cottages near the beach on this side. The cops are still here so that no one sets up again."

"Shit," Derek complained," We'll have to head back to Denman Island and find someplace else to camp."

"Well," suggested the driver, "I can let you set up your tents on my cottage site. My place is along the beach. You just have to make sure that you stay off the beach with your tents or else the cops will be all over you."

"Jeez, thanks," Derek exclaimed as he turned towards Benjamin and continued. "There, we have a place to stay for the long week-end. Perfect!"

Benjamin hadn't been worried one way of the other. After all, Hornby Island was Derek's idea. As far as Benjamin was concerned, any place was good enough as long as it was quiet and away from the situation they had left at Jacqueline's. Benjamin knew that something had been lost there. It wasn't as if they were boyfriend and girlfriend as theirs was a platonic friendship. It had been so easy when neither of them had a significant other to get in the way of friendship. They had been able to be themselves, to be natural, even when naked, without having to worry about what the other was thinking, without the anxieties of whether or not, one was saying the right thing, doing the right thing. But now, it was all gone. Maybe, he thought, a guy and a gal can't really just be friends.

The summer was turning out to be a summer he would rather forget. Everything that had started to fall into place last spring was now falling apart. He was beginning to think that there wouldn't be a job waiting for them at all in Vancouver. As he continued thinking about it, chewing on the dark thoughts and feeling his stomach tighten in the process, he began to lose confidence. Wouldn't Doug have left them a message with the office to let them know? What was it Doug had said about interviews always happening in December? Maybe there wasn't going to be any work until the New Year? These thoughts haunted him as the car made its way towards the driver's cottage.

The woman pulled up in front of her cottage and invited the boys in for tea after showing them where they could set up their tents. Benjamin, lost in his own darkening thoughts, set up his tent while Derek went in for tea. Once the tent was up, he went for a walk along the shoreline, brooding and worrying about what to do next. He knew he couldn't just continue running around the country from campsite to campsite. He was tired of running, and that was what they had been doing in spite of trying to delude themselves that they had simply been on a summer break like a pair of high school kids. Winter was coming. What would he do? What could he do? What could he do until Doug had work for him, if he had work for them? Somewhere, Benjamin knew there had to be an answer and not just the barrage of unending questions.

Lost in his thoughts, he forgot about the passage of time as he walked. It was only with the growing chill in the air that he returned to the reality of his presence on a strange beach with a shiver, which had him finally retrace his steps to his tent in search of a sweater or jacket. He looked up at the darkening sky, at the clouds that were gathering and began to worry about the possibility of rain. When he got back to the tent, he noticed that Derek's tent hadn't been set up yet. Turning to look at the cottage, Benjamin could see through the screen door that Derek and the woman were sitting at the table, eating. He could hear their voices that told Benjamin they were enjoying the meal and each other's' company. Benjamin noticed that a plate had also been set up for him at the table as well. Turning back towards his tent, he found his jacket. Not bothering to put it on just yet, Benjamin made his way to the cottage door and walked in after knocking. Inside the cottage, it was quite warm. There was a fireplace in the next room that was blazing filling the cottage with warmth which felt good after the damp, evening chill along the shoreline.

"Here, sit down and have some salad," encouraged the woman. "You must be starved. I have pork chops on the stove and potatoes and carrots baking in the oven," she added. "By the way, I forgot to introduce myself to you. I'm Faye. Derek told me that your name is Benjamin, Benjamin for short. Which do you prefer? Benjamin or Benjamin?"

"Benjamin, but it doesn't really make a difference," Benjamin responded before saying, "Thanks for the ride and now this meal."

"Benjamin," Derek added, "the weather is supposed to turn Ben by tomorrow. Faye has offered to let us stay in her cottage if we want."

"It's okay," Benjamin returned, "If it's oaky with you, I want to stay in my tent, at least for tonight. You know, sometimes I just want to be alone for a bit. Thanks, Faye, for the offer. I'm not trying to be rude, but,"

"Yeah, I know, Derek said you'd probably choose to stay in your tent. It's not a problem. I just want to make sure you feel free to come into the cottage when it starts raining. I'll leave the door open," she smiled.

Once the meal was finished, Benjamin offered to do the dishes while Derek and Faye sat in the small living room which contained a few small tables, a sofa and three wicker basket chairs. There wasn't a lamp or overhead light in the room, just the fireplace, a few coil-oil lamps and about a half-dozen candles for light. Two of the candles were lit. They were engaged in some small talk while Benjamin was drying the last of the dishes.

Derek suggested that it was time for a bit of music and asked Benjamin if he would play a few songs before he headed back to the tent.

"Or just come and sit with us and enjoy a glass of wine by the fire if you're too tired," offered Faye.

"Thanks for the offer, Faye, but I'm beat. I'll just head out to the tent and go to bed. Thanks again for the supper."

"You're welcome," Faye replied. "Well, we'll see you in the morning for breakfast. Good night, Benjamin."

"Night," Derek chimed in.

"Good night, all," said Benjamin as he walked out the door into the damp and cool night.

Chapter Sixteen

The rain did come just before supper on Sunday, their second day on Hornby Island. It wasn't really rain, but rather more of a light mist falling. So, Benjamin decided to continue sleeping in his tent, at least for that night. Derek was sleeping with Faye and Benjamin didn't want to be in their way. During the night, the rain picked up a bit, drumming incessantly on the tent and Benjamin knew that he would have to either go into the cottage come morning, or leave the island and find a hostel, probably in Nanaimo. His time alone in the tent had given birth to a new idea. He thought he could spend the winter on Salt Spring Island, a place well known for being friendly to strangers, especially those that musical or artsy, the hippies. While there, he would collect unemployment insurance and then head off to South America in the spring time once he had saved enough money. Benjamin had heard of an old city in the mountains of Peru called Machu Picchu, an ancient civilization, which he wanted to see. With the sound of the rain continuing to play on the tent, Benjamin's thoughts began to still and he fell asleep.

When he woke up in the morning, his sleeping bag felt damp. The decision to leave was made, so he took down his wet tent, rolled it up to put beneath his backpack. His sleeping bag was rolled up in a sheet of plastic, but not before it got even damper. Tying the sleeping bag on the top of the backpack and then lifting it onto his back, Benjamin turned for a last look at the cottage. He thought he would just leave, but a wave of guilt washed over him. He rethought his plan and knew he needed to let Derek know that he was leaving and that he would catch up with Derek later.

There were still no signs of anyone being awake in the cottage as he opened the screen door quietly. Putting the backpack just inside the door against the wall, Benjamin walked to the counter and made himself a cup of instant coffee. He sat at the table with the cup of coffee and waited for Derek and Faye to wake up. While waiting he stared out the window at the gray scene. Through the light rain, he saw a truck and two cars pull up to the parking area by the ferry dock. It wasn't long before he saw the ferry pulling in for its first run of the day. It was about an hour later, when Derek and Faye finally emerged from the bedroom, hungry and happy.

"Morning," Faye said to Benjamin, brightly. "I see it's still raining outside and that you've brought in your stuff," she added. "As I said before, you can sleep in the guest room."

"Thanks, but I'll be heading out in a while. I've got a few things I want to check out," Benjamin replied before turning back to Derek and saying, "I'll get a hold of you later, Derek."

"Well, at least wait until you've had lunch with us. Maybe it'll let up a bit in an hour or two," Faye suggested before Derek spoke up.

"Yeah, no problem, man. But. Like Faye says, let's eat first, okay?"

Faye cooked up a batch of pancakes and fried up some eggs for a late breakfast while coffee was percolating on a back burner of the stove. When all was ready, Faye set out the food and poured each of them a fresh cup of coffee. Derek asked Benjamin about his plans. Benjamin talked about checking out Salt Spring Island without mentioning his ideas of staying there. When the meal was done, Benjamin thanked Faye for her warm hospitality and got ready to leave.

At the door, Derek said to Benjamin, "We'll meet up in the city. I'll check with Jacqueline to find out where you are if you're not there at her place when I get there." Derek knew that Benjamin was just giving him space and privacy with Faye. It was just the way Benjamin did things, always considerate and discrete. Derek figured that Benjamin was going to head directly back to the city and Jacqueline's and that the talk of Salt Spring Island was for Faye's benefit.

Benjamin pulled on the backpack after giving his best friend a parting hug. Giving a wave to Faye as he walked out the door along with a final, "Thank you," he made his way towards the ferry. His hat was soon soaked as the rain hadn't let up, but it did help keep some of the rain off his eyes. He had wrapped his guitar case in a couple of plastic garbage bags that Faye had given him. It was enough to keep the guitar dry, but Benjamin knew that he'd have to get out of the rain soon as he was getting chilled.

By the time Benjamin had arrived in Nanaimo he knew it was too late in the day to continue travelling to the town of Crofton where he could catch the small ferry to Salt Spring Island where there were two hostels in which he had hoped to find a bed for the night. With that idea falling apart, Benjamin knew he would have to find a hostel bed in Nanaimo and continue his journey the next day. Tired, hungry, wet and cold, he looked for a nearby restaurant where he could eat and hopefully find out about the local hostel. There was no way he wanted to unroll his wet tent and sleep in his damp sleeping bag. It was now raining quite hard. He spotted a small restaurant, a chain restaurant that he knew served decent food and crossed the road to enter. Once inside, he set his backpack and guitar near the door so that they wouldn't make a mess with the water that was dripping off of them. Then, he sat at a table near the window where he could both look outside at the rain and watch his guitar and backpack. Once settled in, he looked around and noticed that he was the only customer in the restaurant.

Two servers were standing at the back of the restaurant, a young man and woman. Though Benjamin had sat in the young man's section, the young woman put out a hand to her co-worker to whom she stated without any hesitation, "He's mine," in a tone that brooked no argument. Benjamin hadn't followed the exchange between the two servers as he had been staring out the window at the rain. Then picking up a menu, she walked to the table to serve Benjamin.

Chapter Seventeen

She approached Benjamin wearing a brilliant smile that radiated from her eyes to her lips, a smile that seemed somehow out of context with the gloomy, gathering darkness and the constant rain. As she gave him the menu, he noticed her long light brown hair and her eyes that sparkled. He hesitated a moment before noticing that he was staring and that he had to order something.

Flustered, he blurted out, "Coffee. Do you have any coffee?"

"Of course," she answered. "Will you be ordering from the menu?" she asked.

"Uh, yeah, I mean, yes," he nodded still not taking the menu held in her hand.

She gave him a bigger smile and a soft chuckle while waving the menu, saying, "The menu?"

Benjamin sheepishly took the menu. Becoming aware that he was still staring, he quickly lowered his head and made as if he was studying the menu as if it was a final exam, while she walked back to the counter for the coffee. Placing the steaming cup of coffee in front of Benjamin, she retreated to the back of the restaurant to wait until Benjamin was ready to order.

"Did you see him, Gene? I think he likes me," she confided in her partner.

"Marynia! He's drooling. The bugger doesn't stand a chance, why with that big smile you gave him. How come you never look at me like that?" he laughed.

Marynia gave him a small punch to the shoulder and laughed

in response as she re-affirmed, "Just you wait and see. Like I told you, he's mine."

She returned to Benjamin's table and waited while he asked what she would recommend for him to eat, if there was a daily special. It was obvious that he hadn't really seen what was written on the menu which told of the day's specials, Hamburger Steak and Rib Steak. She told him which special she considered to be the best choice. Benjamin had been listening to her voice while he looked at her and hadn't really registered what had been said.

"Well?" she asked expecting an answer.

"I'll take the special," Benjamin replied surprised by the question.

"Which special?" she asked teasing him and distracting him even more.

"Um," he hesitated."

"You mean the hamburger steak and home-made potato wedges?"

"Yes, the steak and wedges," he confirmed with haste.

When she returned a while later with his meal, Benjamin thanked her. She retreated into the depths of the restaurant while he pushed the meat around the platter while nibbling on the potatoes.

"Isn't the steak any good?" Marynia asked with concern returning to his table.

"Uh, yes. Yes it's good, it's very good," Benjamin quickly responded, embarrassed to have her think he didn't like the food. "It's just, um, it's just that I was wondering about the local hostel. I don't want to set up my tent in the rain and I was wondering where the hostel was," he added quickly. He hadn't been thinking about the rain or the hostel at all, but he didn't want her to think it was about the food, and he didn't want to admit what he had been thinking about, that he had been thinking about her.

"Gene?" she called out, "Is the hostel still open?"

"No, it's closed for the season, Marynia. They closed it on Friday so that it can be cleaned so that it's ready for the college students who are heading back to classes."

Benjamin heard her name, Marynia, a strange, exotic name. And then it dawned on Benjamin that he would have to set up his tent in the rain or find a cheap hotel room for the night. Marynia saw the look of disappointment on his face and had a thought. She filled Benjamin's coffee cup and then went to the back of the restaurant and made a phone call.

"Ed, it's Marynia. There's this hitch-hiker who's soaking wet and needs a place to stay for the night sitting here in the restaurant. I was wondering if he could stay in the trailer as the hostel is closed." Waiting while her brother talked to his wife, she looked at Benjamin protectively and possessively. "Yes? Oh thanks so much Ed. I'll be taking him there after my shift is finished here. Love you."

Returning to the table, she sat down beside Benjamin and began to tell him of the trailer and that her brother was willing to let him stay there for the night so that he wouldn't have to set up his tent in the rain.

"Oh, by the way, my name is Marynia and my brother is Ed. He's married and has two kids," she added a bit flustered, surprised at what she had just done. What on earth had come over her? She had just asked a stranger whose name she didn't even know, to spend the night in her brother's trailer. What if he was a druggie?

"I'm Benjamin," he said as he smiled. "Thanks, thanks a million. I was sure that I was going to be sleeping out in the rain. Thanks, Marynia," he repeated saying her name, testing the sound of it in his head, a sound that had a sense of music in it.

The two of them sat together as the evening wore on. Whenever customers came in, Marynia motioned to Gene to take care of them. Finally, her shift was over. She helped Benjamin slip on his backpack as they prepared to leave. Benjamin quickly opened the door with his left hand while carrying his guitar in his right hand. The heavy rains had changed to a light shower, a fine mist that wasn't as cold. At least that was how it felt as Benjamin as he walked beside Marynia who was talking about her niece and nephew and the rabbits they kept as pets in their yard.

Her brother's house was close to the restaurant, only about three blocks away. When they arrived at the street where she lived, Marynia led the way into the back lane and down it past a number of houses. Stopping she opened a gate and waited while Benjamin walked through it with his backpack and guitar. She showed Benjamin the trailer where he was to spend the night. She then asked him to go to the house with her to be introduced to her brother and his family, and get the key for the trailer. Her brother didn't look to happy to see Benjamin. The guitar, the hair and the beard was in sharp contrast to Ed's idea of what a man should look like. Benjamin could tell that he wasn't too thrilled to let a hippie sleep in his trailer.

Turning to his baby sister, Ed said, "He's gone in the morning, rain or no rain. Do you understand?"

"Yes, Ed," she agreed. "Thanks for being such a great brother."

"Don't be long" he said as Marynia led Benjamin back outside, holding the key to the trailer in her hand.

"I'll be back in a bit. I just want to see that everything's okay first," she promised seeing her brother's concern. "It's not like he's not going to bite me or anything," she teased him.

Marynia busied herself with lighting the small furnace while Benjamin set his wet backpack in the garden shed to avoid making a mess in the trailer. He took out a few things that he needed for the night, a tooth brush, and a change of clothes as his were damp, to take to the trailer. When he climbed the two steps to go into the trailer and opened the door, he found Marynia had opened his guitar case and set the plastic bags off to the side. She had put the guitar on the small table on top of a dry towel. She was sitting beside the table waiting for him to enter.

"Can you play a song for me?" she asked.

For the next hour, he played a number of folk songs intent on impressing her, as well as saying thank you to her through the music. He sat on the edge of the bed to play as there was no room between the bench and the table for both himself and the guitar. Marynia joined him on the bed, tucking her legs beneath her as she listened to him play. When he finally stopped to stretch his cramped fingers, they began to talk.

Marynia told Benjamin that she lived on a farm, that she had lived on a farm in Saskatchewan her whole life. Benjamin told her that he lived in Ottawa, not elaborating very much about the fact that unlike her, his family had been rootless living in more than thirty housed in various cities and towns in five different provinces as he group up. Benjamin talked instead of the places he had played music and about his job after high school working for the Federal Government, and about his recent job working as a stock auditor in Vancouver.

With a few more tidbits of their lives swapped while they were holding hands, Benjamin felt himself drawn to Marynia, desperately wanting to hold her in his arms, to kiss her. It was as if there was a magnet that pulled him, that seized him. He found himself getting lost in her, a pleasant kind of lost that felt strangely as if he were returning to a home that had existed long before he had even existed. He wasn't aware that Marynia felt the same strong pull, the same need, the same desire.

While he had played his guitar, Marynia had studied his fingers, his face and his eyes that looked straight into her depths as he sang to her. She knew him, she didn't know how or why. Behind his face there was a presence that was familiar, one that spoke of a connection that seemed to be beyond time. She had always known him though she didn't know how or when they had lost each other. None of it made sense to her practical mind. She only knew the reality that he was here, now, singing to her again. How did this make any sense?

She knew only those people that had crossed the brief twenty years of her life, most of it spent on an isolated immigrant's farm at the very edges of Canadian society surrounded by hills and trees and rocky soil. Yet, in spite of all the facts of never having seen Benjamin before, she knew him, intimately and trusted in that knowledge. There was no way she saw going into her future without him now that he had re-appeared from, and with that thought she stumbled. Yet, she had recognized him the moment he had walked into the restaurant. Now, as Benjamin finished his song to her, she smiled in invitation as he brought her lips to his, holding her face in his hands, she didn't hesitate to welcome him back.

Marynia pulled back carefully, her hand gently pulled his hand that had wandered to touch her swelling womanhood.

"I'm sorry, Benjamin," she apologized. "I can't. I'm sorry, I just can't. I made a promise to myself and though I really want to make love to you with every fiber of my being, I just can't. Not now, not this way." She told Benjamin of her fear of becoming pregnant, about not being on the pill, and that she was a virgin.

"It's okay," smiled Benjamin as he gently kissed her on her lips and moved his hand to again caress her buttocks. "We have the rest of our lives to make love."

She looked at him, her eyes showing momentary surprise at his last statement.

"Will you marry me?" Benjamin surprised himself with those words wondering where they had come from. For some reason he asked knowing that she would say yes, certain of it.

Marynia looked at Benjamin, directly into his eyes. Her heart was telling her, 'Yes! Yes! Yes!' She nodded and then said, "I thought you would never ask. Yes, Benjamin, Yes I will marry you and be yours forever!"

She spent the night with him, laying wrapped in his arms as he lay wrapped in hers, their bodies touching intimately, unclothed beneath the warm feather quilt, their legs entwined. When Benjamin opened his eyes, he saw Marynie staring into his eyes. It was if she had called to him in his sleep, drawing him out of dreams back into life.

"I love you, Marynia," he said with his eyes looking into the depths of her hazel eyes. "Good morning, Beautiful."

Before long, they pulled back from each other. It was light out, daytime. The skies had cleared leaving sunshine as a symbol of benediction for their reunion that was beyond the boundaries of this time and place. Together they talked about the future, not some distant future, but of tomorrow and the days that were to follow. Benjamin had told her that he had a job waiting in Vancouver asking her if she would go with him to Vancouver, that they could catch the afternoon ferry. But before that, before he left to return to Vancouver, Benjamin suggested that they could hitch-hike to Victoria and spend the rest of the morning and the afternoon there, together. There was so much he wanted to show her, so much more to talk about.

Marynia knew that she was in trouble with her brother. She had spent the night with Benjamin rather than return to the house. He would think the worst. She did have to go into the house and get ready for a day in Victoria with Benjamin and she wasn't looking forward to the scene she knew was going to happen.

"I have to talk with my brother and pack my things, Benjamin. I'll go to Vancouver to be with you. But, I need a few days first so that I can leave here the right way. My job, my niece and nephew and my brother and his wife. They've all been good to me, I just can't leave without doing it right. Is that okay with you?"

Benjamin agreed and then asked her if she would still go with him to Victoria for the day before he left on the ferry.

"Yes, Benjamin. I'll go with you. But first, I have to go to the house. I'll be right back. Stay here and wait for me."

She returned after a short delay with a harried look on her face which disappeared when she entered the trailer and saw that Benjamin was still there. They stayed just long enough for Benjamin to get his backpack out of the shed and put the few things he had taken out of it the night before, back into it. With the sun out, Benjamin discarded the plastic so that his sleeping bag would air out. Holding hands, they walked down the lane in the sunshine, to the street and then to the highway that cut through town where they caught a ride to Victoria.

Benjamin showed her parts of the city he had come to know over the late winter and spring. They went into the wax museum and the aquarium exhibit. Even though Marynia had lived on the Island for almost a year, she hadn't got to see much of anything on the island other than camping sites with her brother and his family. It was well after noon when Benjamin realized that they hadn't had anything to eat. Both of them were hungry. He also worried that he had spent a lot of his remaining money during the morning and worried that he wouldn't be able to even pay for a decent lunch. He knew he couldn't pay for a meal and then have enough for the ferry back to Vancouver. And then he remembered the credit card. He remembered it was good for Esso gas stations and their Voyageur restaurants, as well as the Canadian

Pacific Railway hotels such as the Empress Hotel in Victoria. With that thought providing a way out of his dilemma, Benjamin took her to the Empress Hotel for afternoon tea. When they entered the hotel's restaurant, Benjamin showed the person at the door his credit card hoping that it would indeed be accepted by the hotel. The credit card was the key which had the person give a smile and welcome then into the restaurant. Without it, there was little likelihood that they would been allowed inside the hotel. With his long hair and beard, his backpack and guitar, being with a young woman with even longer hair, they looked like hippies, and on

Benjamin's part, indigent hippies.

Marynia looked at Benjamin with a different perspective. Perhaps he wasn't as poor as she first thought. Well not exactly poor, but to have a credit card that allowed them to eat in such a posh hotel, that suggested a level of wealth that was beyond her personal experience. With all she had told Benjamin about herself, she had left out the fact that her family was very poor. A few of her brothers had found work in logging and had escaped the poverty, like Ed. But, life at home on the farm was still a life of poverty. She began to momentarily wonder if her real poverty would make a difference to Benjamin. Then as quick as that thought emerged, it was banished. Of course it wouldn't make a difference.

With the meal done and the payment made with his forging of his father's signature, Benjamin and Marynia walked to the ferry terminal. They stood at the gate for walk-ons to the ferry, talking while waiting till the last possible moment before Benjamin had to go onto the ferry.

"I'll be on the eleven o'clock ferry on Wednesday, Benjamin. Promise me that you'll be there waiting for me," Marynia asked not wanting to have Benjamin leave without her. She knew in her heart that she could trust him, but she didn't know if her heart was more naïve than wise.

"I will be there, Marynia, I promise you. I will be there an hour early just in case you come on an earlier bus. There is nothing that could keep me away. I love you," he repeated for the umpteenth time. The warning horn sounded and Benjamin broke free from the arms that he never wanted to leave.

Part Four

The Magical Other

Chapter Eighteen

The ferry ride back to Vancouver seemed to pass quicker than usual. Once off the ferry, Benjamin hitched a ride into the city and then caught a bus to take him to Jacqueline's. It was almost dark by the time he arrived. The lights were on and he could hear music playing inside of the basement suite. Knocking on the screen door, he waited for a few moments before catching on that no one could hear the knock because of the volume of the music. He looked in and was surprised to see Betty, Linda, and Derek in the room with Jacqueline and Jack. Opening the door and entering, his nose caught the sticky sweet smells of marijuana and hashish.

Derek saw him as he entered and yelled out, "Where the hell have you been, Benjamin? You left before I did."

"I thought you were moving in with Faye on Hornby Island," Benjamin replied. "When did you get here?" he asked in evident surprise at seeing Derek in the apartment.

"This afternoon."

Jacqueline stood up, walked over to Benjamin and gave him a big hug and an even bigger kiss. Benjamin was surprised with the kiss, especially with Jack watching. With no reaction from Jack, Benjamin guessed that he was stoned as well. "Missed you, Benjamin," Jacqueline breathed into his ear.

Stepping back out of her arms, Benjamin looked at her and smiled while saying, "Missed you, too, Jacqueline."

Derek called out, "Jennie! Tell Benjamin what Doug said!"

Benjamin looked questioningly at Jacqueline as she told him about seeing Doug yesterday and begin told that there wouldn't be any work until just after Christmas. No one did inventories after the summer.

"Hi, Benny," giggled Betty who was also higher than a kite. Benjamin waved at her and saw that Linda looked as though she was sleeping on some cushions on the floor beside Betty.

"Hi Betty, good to see you again." Benjamin replied as Jacqueline grabbed his guitar and carried into the room. Benjamin set his backpack by the door, took off his sandals and went to sit on the floor beside Derek. Benjamin was anxious to tell Derek all about Marynia.

"Hey everybody!" Derek called out once he had heard about Marynia, "Benjamin has a girlfriend!"

Benjamin felt embarrassed with Derek's public pronouncement, but also felt good at the same time. The grins spread out around the room told him that the others thought it was pretty good as well. Only Jacqueline didn't seem to show any reaction though it was hard to tell as she was turned away from his view.

"Tell us about her," Betty said while trying to get Linda to wake up.

"Her name is Marynia, repeating what little they already knew," he began. "She's beautiful with long, straight long hair, almost blond hair. She has hazel eyes and she's beautiful."

"You already said that," Derek smirked.

"She's about this tall," he continued holding his hand to just below his nose. "And, she has the most amazing smile. She's just, well, perfect," he grinned. "And, she said yes when I asked her to marry me."

Aside from the sound of music playing in the background, the room went silent with everyone, including Linda looking at Benjamin. It was Derek who was the first to break the stalemate of the silence.

"What the hell did you just say?" asked Derek.

"I asked her to marry me, and she said she would marry me," repeated Benjamin.

"Are you out of your frigging mind? Did you really ask her to marry you?"

"Yeah," answered Benjamin surprised at Derek's response to the great news.

"So, where is this beautiful young woman that said she would marry you? Did you leave her outside?"

"She's still in Nanaimo," admitted Benjamin. "She said she'd come to be with me on Wednesday when I go and pick her up at the bus depot."

"God, Benjamin," said Derek as he shook his head in disbelief. "You're the most naïve person I have ever met. Do you actually think she is going to marry you? That she will be at the bus depot on Wednesday? You're even dumber than I thought."

Jacqueline gave what appeared to be a sigh of relief and sought to bring an end to the tension that was building up between Derek and Benjamin. She was sure that Derek was right about this 'girlfriend,' and let out the tension that had built up within her when she heard about a new girlfriend and marriage. Jacqueline called out to Benjamin to play a few songs for them. "Play some of the old songs we used to sing in the van, Benjamin. Please?"

Still smarting from Derek's rude comment, Benjamin took his guitar from Jacqueline's outstretched hand and soon had them all singing along to their favorite road songs. When he stopped to go to the bathroom, the room settled back down into an almost depressed mood, the drugs had worn off for the most part and there was apprehension about the possibility that Benjamin had told them the truth. When Benjamin returned, he assumed that the news of Doug not having work for them until after Christmas was responsible for the depression. Linda was saying that there was no effing way she wanted to go back to live with her parents and work as a babysitter for the brats next door. Jacqueline talked about looking for work, perhaps a waitress job, so that she could pay her rent until they got back on the road, together in December.

It suddenly dawned on Benjamin that he didn't have a job anymore and he didn't have any money and that Marynia was coming to Vancouver to live with him, thinking that he had a job. She was quitting her job, coming to live with him, depending on him to take care of her. What the hell was he going to do now? Would she go back to Nanaimo when she found out he had no job? The emotions of doubt and despair appeared on his face as he sunk into the cushion he was sitting on. Holding his head between his hands, he forgot about the others around him. As he crouched there Betty touched him on the shoulder to get his attention. Looking up, he saw her give him a weak smile as she handed him a small piece of paper, telling him to put it into his mouth, telling him that it would help.

In the darkness of what appeared to be a swampland, Benjamin felt afraid. He was naked and shaking with cold and fear as he tried picking his way through the knee-deep water. He felt the water come alive and crawl up his legs. Trying to brush off the sticky, smelly but invisible creatures that crawled on him, he began to run and found that he could barely move at all. The creatures began to take on shifting shapes as they crawled over most of his body and touched his face. Huge, black spiders that looked him in the eye, promising him that he would suffer, suffer more than he had ever suffered before. Benjamin screamed.

Jacqueline held him as he continued to scream. Betty's LSD had Benjamin locked into a bad trip. Jacqueline knew it would pass. She'd been there before. Everyone else was too far gone into their own acid trips to help her with Benjamin. All she could do was to hold him and wait. She looked at Benjamin with sadness, wondering why he had never seen her love for him. When Benjamin had left in early July, she had cried for days thinking that he was never going to come back. It was just after the third week when she had lost all hope of Benjamin's return that she had met Jack. He made her laugh. Lonely and depressed, she grasped at this small gift of laughter and so they hooked up. She didn't love Jack. She knew that she never would love him, that he was anything more than someone who filled her lonely bed. She loved Benjamin but didn't know how to tell him that, didn't believe that she was worthy of him loving her back, she afraid that he wouldn't love her back.

Marynia sat crying on the kitchen chair while her brother was yelling at her, calling her a tramp.

"You slept with him in my trailer. Christ, Marynia. What the hell were you thinking?" Ed had been angry from the moment she returned to the house after leaving Benjamin in Victoria. "You think he really loves you?" he threw at her. "Well, have I got news for you. He got what he wanted and he's gone. What if you're pregnant? Jesus, what a frigging mess."

"We didn't have sex," Marynia repeated for what seemed to be the fifth time. "I'm not pregnant. You have to have sex to get pregnant, Ed. Can't you understand? We didn't make love. I'm not pregnant. He loves me, Ed, and I love him."

Sitting straighter she found the courage to continue. "I'm going to Vancouver to be with him. We're going to get married. He loves me and I love him. And, there's nothing you can say to stop me. You're not my father!"

Swearing, Ed turned away in disgust telling his wife, "See if you can talk some sense into her. There's no frigging way she's going to Vancouver to sleep with that long-haired loser."

Still crying softly as she lay in her bed that night, she vowed to herself that she would go to Benjamin. She knew it was going to mean that she'd have to sneak out when it was time to leave for the bus to Vancouver, and that Ed would probably hate her for the rest of his life, but she had to go to Benjamin. She fell asleep with that promise on her lips.

In the morning, after Ed had gone to work, she went to the restaurant and quit her job. Her boss was sad to see her go as she was a popular waitress with the customers. She explained that she was going to Vancouver to live and needed her final pay now if he could give it to her. Handing over the money, he wished her luck and reminded her that if she ever came back to Nanaimo, he would have a job for her. Marynia hugged him as she said goodbye, before turning to her co-workers who were on shift to say her goodbyes to them. Taking the money she had earned, she hurried out the door and returned home, to Ed's home, to pack her suitcase with all the things she wanted to take with her. There wasn't much other than some clothes she had bought for herself with her earnings, and her toiletries. There was no way that her brother was going to stop her, tomorrow.

Benjamin sitting at the table in the kitchen early on

Wednesday morning, having a bowl of cereal and a cup of coffee. Derek had just woken up and was having a coffee with him.

"You're effing crazy, Benjamin. I tell you, it's a waste of time. All you're gonna do is get hurt."

"She'll be there, I know she'll be here." Benjamin said defiantly. "I told you, she loves me. Why can't you understand that?"

"What'll you do if she doesn't show?" Derek challenged.

"It's not going to happen," Benjamin affirmed with conviction. "I've got to go. I don't want to be late and have her think I am not coming."

"You're so stupid, it hurts," Derek complained as he put on his shoes and grabbed his jacket.

"What are you doing?" Benjamin asked.

"Going with you of course, idiot" he replied. "You're going to need me when she doesn't get off that damned bus."

They left carrying the argument out of the door with them, the arguing stopping only when they climbed up onto the bus. They arrived at the Greyhound bus depot early and sat on a bench outside the terminal in the passenger drop-off area so that they could see all the passengers who got off the buses that pulled in from various locations. They were early as Benjamin wanted to make sure she saw him in case she had perhaps caught an earlier bus. The last thing he wanted was to cause her to panic and worry because he wasn't there. When the eleven o'clock bus from Nanaimo finally pulled in, he studied each face getting off, hoping that she was one of the passengers. But, she wasn't on the bus.

Derek didn't make any comments other than to go and get some more coffee. When he returned he handed Benjamin a paper cup filled with black coffee and then sat silently waiting with him for the next bus from Nanaimo. The bus came and disgorged all of its passengers. Marynia was still not on the bus. Benjamin sat still, not daring to take his eyes off the bus, not daring to look at Derek, not daring to say a word. He just sat and stared in silence.

Marynia was in a panic. Ed had stayed home in the morning to make sure she didn't take the bus to Vancouver. She had cried and screamed at him without success. Once it was too late for her to catch the bus, he left for work telling his wife to make sure that Marynia stayed in her room until he got home from work. Now, she was in her bedroom, crying and trying hard to think. She knew that Benjamin would be at the bus station and that he would see that she didn't get off the bus. What would he do when she didn't show up? It all felt so hopeless. Yet, a part of her knew that Benjamin would stay in the bus terminal waiting for the next bus, and the bus after that; he would wait for her. She had to leave, now.

"Let's go," Derek suggested gently once the bus had pulled away from the terminal. "Let's go back to the house, Benjamin."

"I'm not leaving," Benjamin said with conviction. "She's coming. I know it. I'm staying here. She'll be in a panic if I'm not here. She would wait for me if I was the one coming on the bus, I know it."

Derek stayed waiting with Benjamin as another bus came and went before he gave up and left Benjamin sitting on the bench. Nothing he could say had penetrated Benjamin's thick skull. Maybe by the end of the day, Benjamin would realize that it was all just a fairy tale. Derek knew you just couldn't trust a woman, any woman no matter what they said. The safest thing you could do was build a wall around yourself and . . . He didn't complete the thought. He was angry at what a woman was doing to his best friend. He knew Benjamin would give up and come back, he just didn't know when.

It was late in the afternoon when Marynia's bus pulled into the depot in Vancouver. She was four hours late. Would he still be there waiting? Was she worth waiting for? Doubts assailed her, but she beat them back knowing that somehow, he would be there, waiting and believing in her.

The bus pulled into the station and the passengers began to get off. Benjamin watched confident that Marynia was on this bus. For some reason, his mood had lifted as he sighted the bus turning the corner and then slide into its parking stall. As soon as he spotted Marynia behind some of the other passengers, he raced from his bench and was there to take her hand as she stepped down onto the walkway. Without taking another step, they wrapped their arms around each other and cried in relief that the waiting and the niggling negative voices were now banished. Though they were an obstacle around which the rest of the passengers had to bypass, no one was angry. The scene that Benjamin and Marynia presented was one that brought a universal glow to everyone.

"You waited," was all she said before her lips found his.

They took a bus to Jacqueline's place and talked the whole time. Marynia told him about Ed's anger and how he felt betrayed by her. Ed had been her protector, her big brother who loved her. His anger had as much to do with feeling he had failed in protecting her than it was about Marynia's betrayal of his trust. He just didn't know that she had met the right man. There was no way she could explain it to him as she could hardly explain it to herself. How was it possible to know so adamantly that the stranger that walked through the door at the restaurant was the man she was going to marry, that she had to marry?

When she stopped to take a breath, Benjamin told her about the job that had disappeared, that there was no return to that job until after Christmas. He felt ashamed to have to admit that he didn't have much money left either.

She silenced his self-recriminations with a kiss to the lips and then saying, "It'll all work out, don't worry. It'll always work out, Benjamin"

Chapter Nineteen

They had stayed with Jacqueline for the next two nights while Derek and Benjamin searched for their own place to live, a place which they would share so as to keep rent costs down. The job search was also on with Marynia being the first one to get a job working at the White Spot café. The apartment they found was in the same building on Granville where Betty had an apartment. It was cheap and small. When Benjamin showed it to Marynia, he saw the look of disappointment on her face.

The place needed a lot of cleaning and there was only one bed, a big double bed, but still only one bed. Benjamin told her that the landlord was giving them the place for free for the first month as Benjamin had promised to repaint the interior of the apartment and do whatever else needed fixing, all to be done at the owner's expense. It was as good as a job for now until he managed to find one. As for being in one bed, he would sleep on the floor.

Since they weren't going to have intercourse until she got the pill and it had time to work, it shouldn't be a problem. By then they would have their own apartment. With a bit of misgiving, Marynia agreed. She didn't want to spend any more time than she had to in Jacqueline's apartment. She saw from the moment they met, that Jacqueline loved Benjamin. Though Jacqueline had been nice to Marynia, it was obvious that she would rather that Marynia didn't exist.

They had until the end of the month to earn enough money to pay for October's rent. While Benjamin worked long hours over the next few days fixing the apartment, cleaning it of all the silverfish and cockroaches that skittered all over the place, repairing the holes left in the walls by the previous tenant, and painting the apartment, Marynia worked long hours at the restaurant earning more in tips than she did in wages. It was more than enough for food which helped Benjamin prepare. She couldn't believe that he could be so good in the kitchen. He was a much better cook than she was.

When the apartment was finally painted, with ceiling done in a very dark blue with silver stars painted to have it resemble the night skies, she saw another side of him. With the money she had earned in Nanaimo, and the money she would earn at the White Spot restaurant by the end of the month, they would have enough money to pay for the next month's rent. However, she kept that knowledge to herself. It had to do with Derek and the fact that there was only room for one bed in the apartment. Derek had found the apartment and it was rented in his name.

The bed, how could she explain it to Benjamin so that it could make sense? She had convinced Benjamin to lay beside her in the bed, to put distance between her and Derek. As she lay beside Benjamin each night, with Derek on the other side, she wanted so much more of Benjamin than was possible. Benjamin held her and kissed her gently each night but she could feel the tension in him, his need. She worried that he would give up on her as a woman and settle for just being friends. Derek slept nude, and Benjamin wore briefs while she kept on her panties and wore one of Benjamin's tee-shirts in bed. As she lay there in the dark of the night, she felt Derek's arm rest on Benjamin and wondered.

On the third day in the apartment, Derek told Marynia and Benjamin that Linda was moving in as well. That night, in the dark as the four of them lay in the bed pretending to be asleep, Derek and Linda began to make love, quietly at first, but unable to contain it in silence. Benjamin moved closer to Marynia and held her tighter than normal trying to protect her from the uncomfortable reality of what was happening beside them. The sounds, then the smell pushed him even closer. Marynia turned in his arms to hold him closer, to fill in even the small gaps that were left. And, when they woke in the morning, they were still entwined in each other.

By the fourth night, Marynia felt the tension in Benjamin growing. He was less patient and not wanting to play his guitar. She saw the dark clouds passing over his face as bedtime approached. She could tell that as much as she hated sleeping in that bed with the other couple in the bed, Benjamin was finding it even more difficult. She could feel Benjamin disappearing into a dark and deep inner place. As she lay beside him listening to him as he barely breathed in his attempts to control himself, she knew that she had to let go of her own fear. She was more afraid of losing Benjamin than of anything else. She felt his rigid body next to hers as Derek and Linda were again having sex in the bed on the other side of him. Marynia moved to draw him closer then shifted to take his place next to the other couple. Then, she took him into her.

"You're the only man I have ever had sex with," Marynia said as she lay in the bathtub only moments after they had made love, while Benjamin sat in a chair looking at her. Benjamin had wondered at the lack of a blood stain which he had expected with the breach of her hymen. "You have to believe me."

"I do believe you, Marynia. It's okay, I do believe you. Why wouldn't I believe you?"

"But, we can't do this anymore. I don't want to get pregnant. We can't make love until it is safe, until the birth control pills are effective," she said as tears fell. "But, I don't want to lose you, either, Benjamin."

"You're not going to lose me, Babe." Benjamin stated gently

and with certainness. "You're never going to lose me."

Neither Derek nor Benjamin had yet found a job. Derek was drinking heavily and talking about maybe joining the army, the American army, perhaps the Marines if they would let him enlist.

"Yessir," Derek said slurring his words, "them 'Mericans sure could use two fighters like us, eh Benjamin? Whatcha say there pardner?"

Both were drunk, very drunk. Marynia had drank more that she was used to, but she wasn't near as intoxicated as they were.

"Urp!" Benjamin's belch was the only answer he gave to that suggestion before he passed out. Marynia saw her opportunity and took it. She told Derek that he had to find someplace else, somewhere else to live, and someone else besides Benjamin to save his sorry ass.

In the morning, Marynia discovered that Derek hadn't been as drunk as she had thought as Derek told Benjamin about Marynia's trying to break up their friendship. Derek told Benjamin that no woman was worth it. Who had stuck by Benjamin through his tough times, he demanded. Who had bailed him out every time he got into trouble? Derek wasn't aware that he was talking of himself rather than Benjamin, but the words did reach Benjamin.

Benjamin's head and stomach hurt and Derek's words left him hurting in his heart as well. He took all of it in and felt the guilt in not having been a good enough friend, a guilt that pile onto the truth that he was failing Marynia as a man as well as Derek as a friend. What kind of man had his love sleep in the same bed with others? What kind of man couldn't even pay the rent? He looked inside and saw the reflection of his father who had repeatedly failed his mother and his children. Benjamin began to fear that he wasn't going to be any different. The best thing he could do was to disappear and stop causing so much hurt.

Later that day while Marynia was at work, Benjamin walked to the welfare office and asked for a train ticket to take him home to Ottawa. It was either that or they would have to give him enough money to live in the city, to put him on the welfare roll. He knew that the province preferred to pay for the train tickets for indigents rather than put them on the welfare rolls. He remembered his father had put them in this situation in Vancouver when Benjamin was thirteen years old. With the voucher in his hand for a train that was leaving the next evening, Benjamin returned to the apartment. When Marynia returned from her early shift at the restaurant, she saw Benjamin's backpack standing next to the door and began to cry.

Benjamin tried to explain telling her about his father, about growing up on welfare and seeing how he was no better than his father. She deserved so much more than he could ever give her. The words poured out and her tears continued to fall. She knew she had lost him and her heart was breaking.

Later, in the night as they lay one last time beside each other, both fully clothed in the bed alone as Derek had not returned, Marynia said she was going to go home to her parent's farm. Without Benjamin, there was nothing for her in Vancouver. They would take the train together away from Vancouver, and in the end away from each other. In spite of the realization that it was all over, they held each other tightly as though somehow it would be enough to change it all, to make it all better.

They spent the night on the train on their bench seat with only a thin blanket covering them. The train had already passed through Saskatoon. Marynia was getting off the train at the next stop in Watrous, and still they clung to each other hoping that somehow this would all disappear, that they would wake up only to find that it was all some bad nightmare.

As the train finally came to a stop, Marynia let go of Benjamin and picked her suitcase off the overhead rack. She turned again to Benjamin and said, "I'll be here, waiting for you to come home to me. I love you." And then she walked to the entrance, went down the steps and walked to meet a young bearded man who took her into her arms. Benjamin could tell that she was sobbing as the young man looked back at the train with anger at the man who had hurt his sister. Then the train began to slowly pull away, heading back to the family that had taught him darkness.

Chapter Twenty

He had been at the family home for two weeks, living back in his old room under the stairs, back working in an IGA grocery store and giving his mother her share of his wages. It seemed from all outward appearances as if he had never left, never experienced any other possibilities for life. Benjamin didn't need the money anyway. His mother let him have enough for the few things he needed and not much more. There really wasn't anything to save for, no desire for things or experiences outside of the world of work and returning to the house and its predictable chaos which, strangely, was a numbing comfort. He went to work and then returned home to clean up the messes left by his brothers and sisters, and do the chores his mother had abandoned without complaint. Once again his mother had begun to call him a good boy. His father wasn't living at home anymore though he was still working on the house he was constructing with Benjamin's two uncles. Georges and Gordon only helped their father on the weekends as they had returned to school at the end of the summer. Benjamin refused to help his father who didn't really need his help anyway.

Laurent had returned to live in his girlfriend's house, a house trailer in the west end of the city. Benjamin knew about the two half-brothers who lived there though they had never met. Benjamin just didn't care anymore. There was no point in caring, in making any scenes as it never changed anything, never improved anything. All that scenes produced was more backlash from both his mother and father with Benjamin coming out the worst following those scenes.

Not once since his return from Vancouver had Benjamin tried calling Derek's home to see if his mother had heard from him. Nor, had he gone to his grandparents' place. He didn't think he could handle their loving him. He didn't deserve their love. Benjamin began to believe that he deserved the life he was living at home, sometimes thinking that even it was more than he deserved. He saw his brothers and sisters in the house at a distance, not able to effectively hear them or even be with them. He could feel their confusion and sometimes even anger at being distanced.

Benjamin just waited for the end of each day when he could hunker down into the darkness of a quiet house. The desire to play guitar had gone and his guitar sat in its case in the bedroom, not taken out once since his return. Even the pleasure of listening to classical music on the radio was absent. In the darkness and silence he could feel pain and perversely, he welcomed that pain. The only alternative would be forever losing pain in a perpetual darkness. It was only habit and duty that kept that black hole at bay.

A few days before Thanksgiving in October, Benjamin came home from work and saw his father's car in the driveway. Benjamin prepared himself for yet another battle as he walked into the house. The kids were all watching TV, and his parents were upstairs in their bedroom. Drawing a breath of relief, Benjamin headed up the stairs to take a shower before the kids began fighting over the bathroom as they prepared for bed. He took a towel and a change of clothes with him into the bathroom passing the closed door behind which his parents were talking. He could hear them but he couldn't hear the words they were saying as he went into the bathroom.

He spent a lot of time in the shower, trying to get clean but still feeling that in spite of the hot water and soap. Finally he shut off the shower, toweled himself dry, put on the clean clothes and left the bathroom. Benjamin quietly made his way down the stairs. He wasn't hungry any longer so he sat quietly with his siblings in front of the television, not hearing or seeing what was on the television. He was still sitting there in front of the television though his brothers and sisters had gone to bed, when his father came down the stairs. He asked Benjamin to make him something to eat.

"How about some fried baloney and tomatoes?" His father asked.

"Sure, Dad," Benjamin answered without enthusiasm but with proper deference as he was hoping to avoid a conflict. "Do you want some coffee too?"

Getting up from the sofa, Benjamin went into the kitchen to make the meal his father had requested. Benjamin couldn't think of anything to say as his father began talking of finishing the house in a few days. He wanted the job done by Saturday so that he could enjoy the Thanksgiving week-end. He told Benjamin that when the job was done that he would be getting the final payment, a large payment. He was talking about the things he was going to be buying for everyone. It was going to be the most money that he had ever had at one time. Benjamin focused on the food cooking in the frying pan and couldn't think of anything to say to his father.

Benjamin had seen this side of his father many times over the years. When things began to go well for his father, the dreams began to take on a vitality that envisioned a better life for everyone. However, reality always had a way of seeing that vitality crash and burn leaving the dreams to become bitter ashes.

When the simple meal had finished cooking, Benjamin put it onto a plate which he then placed on the dining room table. Benjamin didn't really hear what his father was saying while they sat at the table. His mind was numb. He had learned long ago to shut the doors within himself when pain entered his life.

Benjamin was skilled at dissociating from everything in order to navigate through whatever the world demanded of him. If anyone would have looked closely, they would have seen that beneath the thin veneer of presence, that Benjamin was absent, lost somewhere in an inner space, a dark, inner space.

Benjamin had made both himself and his father a cup of instant coffee which he nursed while his father ate. When Laurent had finished his late evening snack, Benjamin took the dirty plate and cutlery into the kitchen where he put them into the sink while his father returned up the stairs. After washing up the few dishes, Benjamin returned to the living room, sat down on the sofa and stared at the television which was still on. He didn't hear his father leave.

On Thanksgiving Day, Mémère and Pépère came to the house with Benjamin's uncles who had helped his father build the house. Mémère had brought a big turkey and was helping Benjamin's mother in the kitchen with the preparations for the Thanksgiving meal. The kids were boisterous and excited about having company and the promise of a good meal. Try as he might, in spite of forced smiles and doing his best to stay positive, Benjamin couldn't feel anything to be thankful for, to be happy about. He had never told anyone what had happened that resulted in him coming home. His brothers and sisters were simply glad that he was there and his mother was satisfied that he was giving her money and more.

When his siblings asked for songs before the meal, Benjamin took out his guitar from the darkness of the guitar case. It had been three weeks since it was last played and now needed to be tuned first. Then, when it was ready, he played for his brothers and sisters. He played well even if there was no enthusiasm or passion in his playing. He didn't have to worry about singing very loud as the voices of the others filled in. Even his grandparents joining in on some old French folk songs. Soon, the smell of roasted turkey with stuffing was soon followed by Mémère calling out to everyone, "À table! Supper is ready!"

Cheers greeted her announcement as everyone rushed to their spots at the table. Benjamin helped his mother and grandmother put the food on the table before sitting beside Neil. Once everyone was seated, Pépère said grace and then Laurent began to carve the turkey. The chatter was overwhelming. Benjamin found himself forced to focus on his breathing while he fought a descent into a black hole of despair. He didn't hear his father ask him which piece of the turkey he wanted. It was only Neil's poke in the ribs that brought his attention back to the present where he saw his father holding white meat out to him.

"Thanks, Dad. I love white meat," he said with a weak smile. Satisfied, his father turned to serve the others. Benjamin resumed focusing on the people at the table and made the appropriate comments and asked the younger kids a few questions so that they felt seen and heard at the table.

Béatrice helped Benjamin with the clean-up and the dishes. The kids were in bed and the house was becoming quiet. His grandparents and uncles were with his parents in the living room with the talk all about the house that had just been finished.

"I have a boyfriend," Béatrice confided in her brother as she dried the dishes he was placing in the dish rack. "He's a quiet guy, just like you. I think you'd like him, Benjamin."

Smiling at her, Benjamin said," If you like him, I know that I'd like him too. So tell me about this quiet guy, Béatrice."

Benjamin listened as his sister talked about her boyfriend, a young man who sounded rather like an awkward kind of guy.

She told Benjamin that she met him at the restaurant where she worked as a waitress. Hearing this part of her story, he winced remembering what he wanted so desperately to forget. Covering up his pain, he told Béatrice that he hoped he would get to meet this young man who had won her heart. She smiled at him and gave him a kiss on the cheek as she turned to go up the stairs to the room she shared with Suzanne, Justin and Heather.

With the food put away and the last of the cleaning up done, Benjamin went into the living room to be a part of the group. He wasn't going to risk creating a scene by being conspicuously absent.

"The owners have said they will make the final payment in two weeks once the house inspection is done," his father was saying as Benjamin sat on a cushion in a corner of the living room. "The final payment is going to be almost seven thousand dollars. Once the last wages are paid and the last materials bill is paid, there is still going to be enough to given you guys a good bonus," he said to his brothers, Blaise and Bernard. "I couldn't have done it without the two of you."

There were big grins all around. Finally after all the years chasing dreams, Laurent had found something which was going to pay off. They talked of plans for trying to build two houses next year at the same time. Laurent was thinking of putting Blaise and Bernard as foremen, one at each site. The site where they had built a house this year had quite a few other lots ready for development.

The talk then turned to the recent kidnapping of Pierre Laporte in Quebec by the FLQ, and how Trudeau was going to deal with it. Benjamin had been following the news about the FLQ for almost two years because of their bombing of the Montreal Stock Exchange and a riot at McGill University. Pépère said that Trudeau needed to bring in the army and hunt them down to the last man.

The conversation started to wear out as the evening grew late. Blaise was driving Pépère and Mémère home while Bernard was heading back to his girlfriend's place for the night. As usual, Mémère gave Benjamin's cheeks a pinch before she kissed him on the cheeks as she stood at the door waiting for Betsy to bring her coat.

"Benjamin, you will come to visit Pépère and I, won't you?" she asked.

Benjamin gave her a hug as he told her, "Oui, Mémère, I'll come and visit you, soon."

When all had left, Laurent turned to Betsy and told her that he would be back the next day; that he had to get a few things from the suppliers early in the morning before he headed to the site. She smiled at him and kissed him good night saying supper would be ready for him the next day.

Of course, he didn't return as he had promised. Each day that he remained away, Betsy's mood become more and more sour. She rarely left her room and still managed to terrorize everyone. Benjamin took it all in without protest. He deserved it. There was no point in pretending that it was ever going to be any better. Each day he would return to the house and find his brothers and sisters in various stages of fear and terror. Benjamin felt helpless. He couldn't go to work and protect them at the same time. Not going to work wasn't an option either. That was made very clear, more than very clear.

One night, after all had gone to bed, he sat alone in the darkness and thought it all just had to end, that there wasn't any point in anything. Somehow, the pain just had to stop.

Chapter Twenty-One

It was near the end of the third week of November when Laurent reappeared at the farm house. He came in like a conquering hero passing out presents to each of the kids and gave a big gift to Betsy who immediately fussed over her husband. It was obvious that he had finally received the final payment from the owners of the house. He called Georges and Gordon into the living room where he was sitting in his favorite armchair as if it was a king's throne.

"Gordon," he began as he held out an envelope, "This is for you for helping me during the summer. It isn't much, but maybe more than you had hoped for." Gordon quickly tore open the envelope and found fifty dollars, a huge windfall for a boy still in elementary school.

Then, turning to Georges, Laurent held out another envelope. "Georges, you worked like a man, you're smart and you aren't afraid to take chances. Here, take this, son." Georges was surprised by the praise from his father. Laurent rarely gave out praise for anything, especially to his children. "Go on," his father urged, "Open it."

Georges looked at the envelope for a few more moments before daring to carefully open it. He saw what was in it before anyone else could and his eyes opened wide in surprise. There had to be more than a hundred dollars there. "Go on, count it. See how much there is there," urged his father. Georges counted out two hundred and fifty dollars. With tears running down his face, he quickly hugged his father and thanked him over and over again.

Laurent smiled at his wife and indicated with a nod of his head that they should go up to the bedroom. He had one more gift to deliver.

It was dark and the house was quiet when Laurent came quietly down the stairs. Benjamin had been sitting in the darkness unable to go to sleep, so he saw his father descending the stairwell, and assumed that he was on his way out the door. It was with surprise, that he heard his father quietly call out his name.

"I'm here, Dad, in the living room."

"Why don't you have a light on?" Laurent asked.

"I don't want a light on," Benjamin responded defensively, ready for an argument knowing that somehow his father would find fault with him. "Are you leaving already?" Benjamin asked with a hint of disgust in his voice.

"No, I'm not leaving, I was hoping you'd leave," he replied.

Benjamin began to panic. Was he losing even this small, last bit of his life? What had he done now to be thrown out of the family home? What had his mother said?

"You're probably wondering why I didn't give you anything earlier," Laurent spoke into the darkness.

"No, not at all. Why would you give me anything? I didn't do anything to deserve something from you. I never helped with the house," Benjamin was quick to answer, hoping that if he was more respectful, that he wouldn't be thrown out, that his father would take back the part where he had said he hoped that Benjamin would leave.

"I want to ask you something," Laurent said with a hint of impatience and even the edge of anger in his voice. "Do you think you could set aside your bitterness, your attitude towards me long enough to talk with me?"

"Yes, Dad. I'll answer any question you want to ask me," Benjamin responded barely able to contain a growing fear,

"I want to ask you about the girl you left in the west." Laurent began."

"Woman, Dad. She's a woman," Benjamin responded defensively

"I want to ask you about the woman you left in the west," he continued. "Do you love her?"

"Of course I love her," Benjamin asserted and puzzled by this line of questioning. "Why are you asking me that?"

"Listen son, don't talk; please just listen. I once had a dream to build a life in the west. That dream didn't work out. I don't know if you know it, but I fell in love in the west when I was a teen-ager, when you were not more than a baby. I gave up that dream to return to Ottawa and try being a good father. I failed over and over again as you know. I failed you, then I failed your brothers and sisters and so many others.

"You don't belong here, Benjamin. You belong with the woman you love, in the west. Don't make the same mistake that I made getting sucked back in to this hellhole. If I had of kept to my dream, perhaps it would have been better for you. You've been paying for my mistake as much as I have."

Holding out an envelope, Laurent gave it to his son. "Go on, open it."

Surprised more by the words his father had spoken than by the envelope now handed to him, Benjamin accepted the envelope and opened it. Inside was a train ticket and two hundred dollars in cash.

"Go son, go to her and don't come back except to visit, and even then, wait for a few years until you get your confidence back and you're strong enough to be able to leave after the visit. There is nothing here for you in Ottawa. Go take a chance on love."

Benjamin couldn't believe that this was his father who was speaking. He looked again at the ticket which was made out for Vancouver. He realized that he hadn't told anyone that Marynia was in Saskatchewan. All they knew was that he had been in Vancouver and that he had left Vancouver to come back home.

"If she really loves you, she'll be there waiting for you, Benjamin. Give her a call. Do you have her phone number?"

"Yes, Dad," he whispered hardly daring to believe that he was having this talk with his father, that he had been given a ticket to go to Marynia.

"Call her, now. Benjamin, call her and tell her."

Benjamin took the phone his father handed to him and called the number he had memorized but had never dialed. A man's voice answered. When he asked for Marynia, there was a pause before the man asked, "Are you Benjamin?"

"Yes, I'm Benjamin. Can I talk to Marynia, please?"

"I don't know if she wants to talk with you," the voice said with more than a little bit of anger.

Benjamin could hear Marynia in the background. "Give me the phone, Brad."

"Marynia?" Benjamin asked, "Can I come back? Will you take me back? I love you, Babe."

"Of course, I told you that when I got off the train, don't you remember? When are you coming?"

Looking at his father and seeing his smile reflected, he answered. "I leaving here first thing in the morning. Can you meet me at the train?"

"Yes, Benjamin. I'll be there, waiting for you. I knew you'd be coming back home to me. Thank you. I love you."

With dawn barely making an appearance, Laurent drove his eldest son to the train station and waited with him for the train's arrival from Montreal. Neither of them had gotten any sleep during the night as they both worked hard be rebuild a father-son relationship. There was so many scars that remained, but there was a whisper of a hope that one day, someday, they would be okay.

Giving his father a final hug, Benjamin thanked him for the ticket and money, but more importantly for the push that was leading him back to Marynia. For all of his father's lifetime of errors, this was enough.

The train pulled into the station at Watrous. Benjamin had to give the conductor advance notice as the train would have continued on to Saskatoon as no one else was getting off at that station. The surrounding prairies were covered in white snow and it was cold, colder that Benjamin had expected it to be. He was shivering as he began to get off of the train, shivering from anxiety as much as from the cold. And then he saw her, waving at him. She was smiling. That smile lit a warmth in Benjamin that banished the cold and his anxieties. Trying hard not to run, he walked up to her, set his guitar and bag on the ground, and wrapped his arms around her not the least embarrassed by the tears that began to fall.

"Welcome home, my love," were her only words as he smothered her next words with a kiss that took both of them into a new world, a new life.

Afterword

As this story was written, or should I say as it was writing itself through me, I became aware of how this story of an individual became a story of a culture. One could read this story as a tale of a number of individuals that serve as stereotypical examples of that culture. Or, one could read this story as one in a long line of fairy tales that talk about how the human psyche is transformed with each character standing in the place of various human complexes and archetypes.

The year I was born, Joseph Campbell wrote a book called <u>The Hero With a Thousand Faces</u>, which traces the same descent into darkness that then propels a person onto a long journey, a heroic journey, where the forces of darkness are overcome. Campbell looked to the stories that have been with us for millennia and sifts through them to trace out the universal, or the archetypal, journey that individuals take to become conscious beings, mature beings.

One of the things I learned from Campbell and a depth psychologist called Carl Jung who wrote Symbols of Transformation, a psychological study of the hero, a hundred years ago, was that once the journey has reached its end, it is somehow transformed into yet another journey. This story finds itself in the same position once one reaches the last page, the realization that "happily ever after," is not what comes next. But rather, a new beginning with another complex journey to follow.

And so, I leave you with this – I will return with the journey that follows the one you have just read.

- Robert G. Longpré, November, 2013

Acknowledgments

No story can come into existence without the direct and indirect influences of others. I do have to give credit to the National Novel Writing Month organisation which gave me a reason for finally sitting still long enough for the novel to come into existence in print form. The story had been buried, unspoken and unwritten for many years. Now, in my retirement, I have no more excuses to keep the story buried.

I must also thank my wife who gave me the encouragement to write this story. My need for quiet time in my study was honoured and protected by her. Of course, as I gave her bits and pieces to read as the novel grew, she was honest in her opinions, something any writer needs if a story is to be worth reading.

I want to thank as well, two people who have read the novel, pointing out various errors in grammar, logic and spelling while also encouraging and supporting along the way. Thank you, Bill and Victoria.

And strange as it might sound, there are a good number of people who have left comments on various bits and pieces of the story that was posted to my blog site. Their words have also spurred me on to write with determination.

And finally, I want to thank you, the reader, for making it to the end of this journey down a broken road. That more than anything else, is what motivated me to write the story, and motivates me to begin the story that will grow out of this one.

About the author

Robert G. Longpré is a retired educator and psychotherapist who lives in Elrose, Saskatchewan, Canada with his wife of more than forty years. He is father to three children, and grandfather to six incredible grandsons. The question of what to do with the shift from working for a living to retirement left the question, 'Now what?' to be answered. The answer grew out of a lifetime of writing on the side for pleasure, and sometimes (perhaps too often) for personal self-therapy.

Robert began writing and publishing while a teenager in Ottawa, the city of his birth, with the co- production of a literary journal called, Left of Center. Poetry and essays of protest found a ready audience during the late sixties. A few years later, Robert turned to publishing small editorials in small town newspapers in Saskatchewan before turning to writing social history and various chapters of educational books that focused on computer-mediated communications, educational reform, and strategies for learning a second language. Since retirement, a number of books that formed a series called, Through a Jungian Lens, were published focusing on Jungian psychology and photography. As well, Robert has maintained a prolific body of blog posts.

This book is the second in the series, Healing the Soul, Skyclad, which is based on the idea that naturism can serve as one option for healing the soul and the psyche. One doesn't heal if one buries trauma under layers of denial. One has to expose trauma and come to terms with that trauma as it has shaped one's life and will continue to shape that life in spite of any conscious intentions. Hiding and denying leaves one crippled in spirit and soul.

Made in the USA
Charleston, SC
18 May 2016